Candid and Compassionate Feedback

Too often educational leaders are caught in a "culture of nice," finding it difficult to give their teachers and staff critical feedback to improve their practice. This important book helps leaders become both candid and compassionate, unrelenting and supportive, demanding yet caring. Exploring real scenarios and situations, this book helps you through the common traps of trying to improve performance, and the strategies to move beyond these pitfalls to achieve desired results. Addressing best practices for driving change such as informal feedback mechanisms, collaborative decision-making, and teacher leadership, this important book will help you create a trusting and supportive environment where you can have candid educational conversations in person and in writing, during informal chats, in PLCs, and with other leaders.

Joseph Jones is the Director of Assessment and Accountability in the New Castle County Vocational-Technical School District, Delaware, USA. He is a cofounder of TheSchoolHouse302, a leadership development institute.

T.J. Vari is the Assistant Superintendent of Secondary Schools and District Operations in the Appoquinimink School District, Delaware, USA. He is a cofounder of TheSchoolHouse302, a leadership development institute.

Other Eye On Education Books Available from Routledge
(www.routledge.com/eyeoneducation)

Five Practices for Improving the Success of Latino Students: A Guide for Secondary School Leaders
Christina Theokas, Mary L. González, Consuelo Manriquez, and Joseph F. Johnson Jr.

Leadership in America's Best Urban Schools
Joseph F. Johnson, Jr, Cynthia L. Uline, and Lynne G. Perez

Leading Learning for ELL Students: Strategies for Success
Catherine Beck and Heidi Pace

The Superintendent's Rulebook: A Guide to District Level Leadership
Patrick Darfler-Sweeney

The Hero Maker: How Superintendents Can Get their School Boards to Do the Right Thing
Todd Whittaker

Bravo Principal!: Building Relationships with Actions that Value Others, *2nd Edition*
Sandra Harris

Advocacy from A to Z
Robert Blackburn, Barbara R. Blackburn, and Ronald Williamson

20 Formative Assessment Strategies that Work: A Guide Across Content and Grade Levels
Kate Wolfe Maxlow and Karen L. Sanzo

7 Steps to Sharing Your School's Story on Social Media
Jason Kotch and Edward Cosentino

Rigor in Your School: A Toolkit for Leaders, *2nd Edition*
Ronald Williamson and Barbara R. Blackburn

Lead with Me: A Principal's Guide to Teacher Leadership, *2nd Edition*
Anita Pankake and Jesus Abrego, Jr.

Candid and Compassionate Feedback

Transforming Everyday Practice in Schools

Joseph Jones and T.J. Vari

Routledge
Taylor & Francis Group

NEW YORK AND LONDON

First published 2019
by Routledge
52 Vanderbilt Avenue, New York, NY 10017

and by Routledge
2 Park Square, Milton Park, Abingdon, Oxon, OX14 4RN

Routledge is an imprint of the Taylor & Francis Group, an informa business

© 2019 Taylor & Francis
The right of Joseph Jones and T.J. Vari to be identified as authors of this
work has been asserted by them in accordance with sections 77 and 78 of
the Copyright, Designs and Patents Act 1988.

All rights reserved. No part of this book may be reprinted or reproduced or
utilised in any form or by any electronic, mechanical, or other means, now
known or hereafter invented, including photocopying and recording, or in
any information storage or retrieval system, without permission in writing
from the publishers.

Trademark notice: Product or corporate names may be trademarks or
registered trademarks, and are used only for identification and explanation
without intent to infringe.

Library of Congress Cataloging-in-Publication Data
A catalog record for this title has been requested

ISBN: 978-1-138-60908-2 (hbk)
ISBN: 978-1-138-60915-0 (pbk)
ISBN: 978-0-429-46635-9 (ebk)

Typeset in Optima
by codeMantra

This book is dedicated to our wives, Vicki Jones and Andreina Vari, for their enduring support of our work.

Contents

Contents

Foreword

For true achievement to occur in our schools, we have to ask the hard questions about what we do, why we do it, and how we can make ourselves and others better. The authors and I know that we must ask these tough questions regularly of ourselves and our colleagues. We've worked together for years as principals and district-level administrators in the state of Delaware. We've presented together in school districts and at major conferences, and have often discussed improving our schools with teachers and principals, or anyone who will listen. These discussions usually take place in hotel lobbies and airport security lines but they all focus on the same issue, creating the desire and passion to produce change in our schools and districts. T.J. and Joe are showing educators around the country how to do just that and have now blessed us with this book to allow us to dig deeper and get even more connected to the work that we know must be done.

I have visited and learned from educators and students from around the world, and I have come to realize that all great schools blend care and compassion with the technical expertise it takes to be effective school leaders, teachers, and staff who make a huge impact on children. Joe and T.J. deliver both in this book, tackling the difficult, and often avoided, topic of candor.

When they first told me that they were writing a book about how successful school leaders know, understand, and use candid feedback as an improvement strategy, I told them to do it quickly as the lives of so many children and teachers will depend on it. The education community simply can't wait any longer for a roadmap to building real trust by confronting our opportunities with a direct path forward. I've said for too long now that so much of our time is spent on the wrong types of accountability measures, and we need to get back to what we know works in classrooms and schools. This book personalizes the concept of holding everyone to a standard of excellence by having candid conversations through a lens of compassion for the people doing the work. As principals, we must understand that one of the greatest ways to influence our teachers is to help them improve their practice.

In this groundbreaking book on candor and authentic conversations, you'll see how the authors demonstrate that our typical best practices—informal feedback to teachers, shared decision-making, and teacher leadership—are indeed the most important strategies for school improvement, but won't be effective unless we are candid with one another. They show us specifically how we sabotage our own success through our unwillingness to be direct and what they refer to as being "trapped in the circle of nice." They illustrate how this is not the fault of any ill intention or lack of care, but rather the result of a breakdown in clear communication and what it means to lead through candor and compassion, especially when our efforts are not yielding results. If we don't challenge ourselves to focus on candor, we won't change!

Candid and Compassionate Feedback: Transforming Everyday Practice in Schools is about outcomes and how we can have direct conversations with people grounded in love and support. Most importantly, this book has practical stories that show us how we limit our effectiveness and what we can do differently in the future. Joe and T.J. willingly tackle one of the most important issues that is holding many schools and businesses back—clear and direct communication with the people on the front lines, in meetings when critical decisions are being made, and in our desire to create leadership pipelines to manage the massive workload of every school community.

I don't just recommend this book, I believe deeply that it should be in the hands of every school leader and teacher (new and experienced), in every school and district in our nation. The practical step-by-step approach to improving communication makes this a must-read, and I hope that this book becomes required reading for every aspiring leader, regardless of profession. I will continue to follow the passionate leadership of Joe and T.J. and their work with the growing leadership institute, TheSchoolHouse302, and I hope you'll join them in starting an education revolution so that students benefit from better communication and relationships, and stronger school cultures!

Salome Thomas-EL, Award-winning principal, speaker, and author

Preface

This book is designed to influence daily leadership practices in schools and districts. The primary audience is principals and principal supervisors, but we firmly believe that anyone who wishes to improve practices in schools for the betterment of student achievement will appreciate this work and the basis for our coming to the conclusion that candor and compassion are the only things that can truly make a difference. The format of this book allows for readers to move around and read from the parts that are most appropriate for them and their development. That being said, it is necessary to read this Preface and the Introduction (Chapter 1) to understand the concepts throughout and how we define certain words to describe our current situation in schools. After that, you can choose to read chapters independently. The idea is simple in that we believe the lack of candor in schools and school systems traps us in a circle of nice, which limits effectiveness and stifles growth. We believe that many educators, regardless of their position, are not candid for two reasons: 1) Fear of offending others; 2) Lack of communication skills on how to be candid without being offensive. Unfortunately, because of our behavior, our lack of candor, we create an environment whereby we continue to accept the status quo in our schools and districts. This creates a "culture of nice" (Ashkenas, 2010; O'Toole & Bennis, 2009; MacDonald, 2011) in which any critical sentiment is taken as offensive. Through respectful candid communication and compassion for one another, we believe we can break out of the circle and realize tremendous individual and organizational growth.

This book is grounded in the premise that three leadership strategies are at the forefront of school improvement efforts and already present as pillars within the school culture. First, we believe that instructional rounds and walkthroughs as informal feedback structures for instructional improvement are critical to success in schools, and we know that teachers and principals are embracing the fact that frequent and quality feedback is necessary for classrooms to flourish. Second, the power of professional learning communities is immense. Cooperative lesson development, data analysis, and shared decision-making are simply critical for breaking down the typically isolated scenarios in schools. Third, teacher leaders and leadership teams are needed if any initiative is going to be sustainable. These three constructs are necessary for success in schools, and this book demonstrates how each can be maximized through a candid and compassionate approach to using them. For that reason, after the Introduction (Chapter 1), each part of the book is set up to address these three best practices for school leadership—informal feedback, shared decision-making, and teacher leadership.

It is also important to note that this book creates a symbiotic relationship between the technical and cultural aspects of work in schools. It's the culture of an organization that houses the improvement we seek. It's also the culture that can hold the organization back from real progress. We firmly believe that school and district culture is a result of the leadership capacity of those at the top of the organization as environmentalists or culturalists in an effort to create an organizational *feel* that drives improvement at every level. The feeling people get at work, their beliefs about what they do, and their willingness to do more than their title or job description *is* culture. We contend that a candid approach embedded within school and district culture is the only way to continuously improve, and we address that in every part of this work.

We wrap candor together with compassionate feedback because we believe that candor is a tool for demonstrating compassion for people. When leaders are candid, acknowledging problems and working to address them through support and change, they are acting with extreme care at the same time. The opposite is true as well. When leaders don't address issues, especially in circumstances where they are obvious to everyone, the leader is communicating that they don't care. It's only when we provide the necessary and candid feedback to our people that they can grow to be the best versions of themselves. That's how leaders show their compassion for their people, by being straightforward and confronting issues as they arise. In this book, not only do we address the importance of candor, but we also demonstrate how you can improve your approach as a school leader.

We hope you find several aspects of this book to be both informative and useful. The Introduction (Chapter 1) sets the stage for how we arrived at the circle of nice. Each part thereafter takes readers through the importance of using best practices in the best way, and then demonstrates the problem with a lack of candor and precisely how to fix it through better language and stronger communication. As a feature of each part of the book, we created a model of success so that leaders can see exactly how all of the components of our best practices work together systematically. Our hope is to present simplicity where schools often find the work to be complicated. Following the models, we provide three scenarios for each of the best practices—informal feedback, shared decision-making, and teacher leadership—and each one is accompanied by both a technical tip for implementation and what we call "Candor Cancellations," which are archetypes of leaders who cancel candor through their own beliefs and behaviors. And, the best aspect is that you don't need to read this book from cover to cover if one part or another stands out as a need for your team.

So why don't you need to read this book from front to back in a linear fashion? We understand the intricacies of teaching and learning and so we designed each part as a distinct concept, developed independently from the other concepts. Our goal is that this book meets the situational demands in your organization and that the various parts can be used independently in a variety of fashions and forums, from book studies to professional development to personal growth. The three parts are simply the most well-documented professional practices in schools—feedback to teachers, professional learning communities for shared decision-making, and teacher leadership. We hope to bring a new lens to each so that they are working at their maximum effectiveness, but we've seen how they can be ineffective without the right culture of trust and candor. This book will get you out of the circle of nice and on your way to a stronger school culture so that you can make immediate improvements to practices. But before diving right into the practices, we want to address how we got trapped in the circle of nice in schools with our Introduction (Chapter 1) to this work.

Meet the Authors

Dr. Joseph Jones is the Director of Assessment and Accountability, overseeing critical elements of teacher and student achievement in the New Castle County Vocational-Technical School District. In 1996, Joe started his teaching career as a social studies teacher at Newark High School in the Christina School District, in the same district where he received his own education. In 2002, he accepted an assistant principal role at a sister school, Christiana H.S. In 2005, Joe left CHS and the Christina School District for a position at Howard High School of Technology as an assistant principal. After a year there, he was selected to be the principal of Delcastle Technical H.S. and served as principal for seven years. During that time, Delcastle received a variety of accolades, and most importantly closed the achievement gap, earning the distinguished honor of being the first high school to receive the Delaware Academic Achievement Award. Joe completed his doctorate in 2007 from the University of Delaware after receiving his masters from Wilmington University in 2001. Joe also works beyond the K-12 setting as an adjunct instructor on topics of school leadership for several universities, and he cofounded TheSchoolHouse302, which is a leadership development institute.

Dr. T.J. Vari is the Assistant Superintendent of Secondary Schools and District Operations in the fastest growing school district in Delaware. He is a former middle school assistant principal and principal and former high school English teacher and department chair. His master's degree is in School Leadership and his doctorate is in Innovation and Leadership for which he accepted an Award for Academic Excellence given to one doctoral student per graduating class. He holds several honors and distinctions, including his past appointment as President of the Delaware Association for School Administrators, his work with the Delaware Association for School Principals, and the honor in accepting the Paul Carlson Administrator of the Year Award in 2015. His efforts span beyond the K-12 arena into higher education where he holds adjunct appointments at three universities, teaching courses at the masters and doctoral level. He is a national presenter on topics of school leadership and the cofounder of TheSchoolHouse302, a leadership development institute.

Their Work Together

Joe and T.J. work together on a number of endeavors. They started *The-SchoolHouse302*, which is a leadership development institute with publications on the topic of leadership and contracted services to support leaders and leadership development nationally. *TheSchoolHouse302* also features blog posts, podcasts, and videoblogs at theschoolhouse302.com, always with a focus on leading better and growing faster. Joe and T.J. have created and delivered professional learning experiences across a wide spectrum of topics all with a focus on leadership development, personal growth, and technical expertise. Both Joe and T.J. graduated from the Executive Leadership Academy through the University of Delaware and they've served (in separate terms) as the President of Delaware's Administrators' Association, including time spent on a planning committee for professional development for the state's educational leaders. They have several past and forthcoming publications that focus on organizational culture and excellence in leadership.

Introduction

The Circle of Nice

How Did We Get Here?

On the surface, a culture of nice sounds good. What could possibly be wrong with being nice? This is especially true in education where we often harp on being cooperative, collaborative, and communicative. The problem is not isolated to being nice, rather it is the absence of being candid. A culture of nice unintentionally creates an isolation from ideas and from feedback. Isolation from feedback creates the subsequent belief that our work is in good order because no one is saying otherwise. When this environment is the norm, and someone comes along with a critical notion, we can get offended. In other environments outside of schools, the notion of critical feedback is what drives performance, and, as such, improvements to practices (Catmull, 2014). We're saying that in the case where this—getting better at what you do through critical feedback—is not the norm, real growth is stifled. It's important to note that education, however, is built on feedback. Every day we give students both formal and informal feedback on their work and progress. We build supports, opportunities, and extra time for them to reach new heights and learn. We are simply advocating for the application of this same model for professionals. We encourage students to have a growth mindset and we need to have one as professionals as well.

A lack of candor is an organizational issue that isn't new, unique, or specific to schools. O'Toole and Bennis called for greater transparency among organizational leaders to meet the growing complexities and demands of industry in 2009. Ashkenas (2010) told readers that the candor problem resulted from "conflict avoidance." Both *Harvard Business Review* works are accurate, yet they don't address schools. The problem is just as extensive and just as convoluted in schools. Similar to businesses, schools continue to operate in systems and structures designed to meet demands that was necessary 60 years ago. As our world has evolved, so must our practices. Candor, guided by a willingness to grow and face the constant challenges in today's schools, is the only way to thrive in an ever-changing society.

Teaching is a complex and tough job. Being a principal of a school is a real challenge; the superintendency is often under fire from every angle. We validate the fact that hard work is being done in America's schools. None of what we report in this book is in any way meant to downplay the hard work that school teachers and school leaders do or to say that schools aren't achieving at various levels of success. Instead, what we're saying is that the environments in schools tend to be places where most people are so intent on being nice and "supportive" of one another that they are not truthful for fear of being labeled as "too opinionated" about how they feel. And, in some cases, teachers and leaders don't know what to feel or how to communicate how they are feeling, which is creating silos, among other problems. Teachers can spend a career in the classroom with only a few worthwhile visits from supervisors and colleagues. Principals can spend years running a school with very limited visits from district office personnel. When this happens, any culture of continuous improvement is eroded by isolation, communication is limited, and people feel lonely and disengaged.

Despite the nature of schools not fostering a culture of candid and compassionate feedback, we contend that through specific strategies and techniques grounded in a culture of vulnerability, schools can flourish. We also believe that this is more challenging than ever given the constant rhetoric that our schools are failing. Let's face it, public school systems have been under attack since the launch of Sputnik and the arms race. The Crisis in Education, as titled by *Life* magazine, was just the beginning of the perception of failing American schools that was only reinforced by *A Nation at Risk*, and ongoing policies that attempt to mandate best practice with little consideration for logistics, finances, or resources. With schools being a constant and easy target, how could we be critical of each other within the organization? *Insiders* (those of us working in school systems) are almost forced to protect one another from any and all harsh comment based on what we know and feel about what *outsiders* (those not working in schools) say. This is exactly what creates a culture of nice that can actually thwart any honest criticism that is necessary to make changes to improve practice. So in our effort to protect each other, our schools, and our systems from the outside world, we fall into a trap where fear prevents us from communicating about the areas that require improvement. This circle of protection draws a clean line around our schools in which we resort to "being nice."

In this book, we don't intend to touch much more on the machine of federal regulation and political rhetoric. That's not our purpose. We only mention it here to uncover some of the context around why candor is so difficult and how the circle formed around our system with nice at the center of it all. Again, educators are working hard in schools. We believe that the American public school system is doing better than it ever has and the data supports that (Ravitch, 2014; Berliner & Glass, 2014). But, we think things can be even greater with the use of candid conversations embedded in what have been labeled as "best practices." In fact, we don't like the word "best" unless these practices are used in the best way. The practices outlined in each part of this book are more like *common* practices unless they are used in the most optimal manner. We're saying that in the absence of candor, these practices are simply strategies used under the veil of "best practices." This book dissects the problem with the lack of candor for each strategy, demonstrates by example what the problem looks like and how to fix it, and then describes what leaders should do to sustain a culture of candor and compassion for each practice. But, before we dig too far into the practices, let's understand more about what it means to be candid and compassionate as a vehicle for positive results.

Our Work in Schools, Districts, and Preparing Leaders

This book was born from our experiences as teachers, department heads, assistant principals, principals, and within our current positions within district offices supporting schools. We have filled many traditional roles within the K-12 system and along the way have challenged the status quo to create environments dedicated to improvement. As we progressed in our careers and achieved various results, we realized one subtle truth that many educators already know—it's the people that make the difference. Policies and programs are only as good as the people who put them into practice. Digging deeper, we realize not only is it the people, but it is the relationships that the leader has with those she leads. However, this is also the crux of where we discovered the difference between what Jim Collins coined as the good being the enemy of the great. Great leaders work tirelessly within those relationships to improve practice. The relationship isn't the end result, in fact this is what can trap leaders in the circle of nice. Rather, it is being able to work within trusting relationships that allows great leaders to achieve results because of the candor that the relationship can withstand.

The schools we were put in charge of were being threatened by possible accountability sanctions under No Child Left Behind. Years of being labeled "under improvement" threatened the schools and change was necessary if not imposed upon us. These schools faced many of the challenges afflicting schools throughout our nation and world with poverty often at the forefront of the proposed issue for students. But leaders don't make excuses and so we influenced change in a positive way that made the difference for the school, for students, and for the people who work in our systems. Joe was the principal of a Title 1 high school for seven years and instituted multiple ideas, initiatives, and programs. T.J. was principal of a middle school that found itself under review from the state department when students weren't meeting their targets for growth toward proficiency. When we took over the schools in our respective situations, we realized that the schools had many of the necessary elements for success, including hard-working teachers who were willing to make changes for the sake of the students. However, the existing initiatives and daily practices could simply be implemented to a better degree, managed and supported more effectively. It was evident that the schools had many of the touted best practices in place, but these practices suffered in environments that did not support candor and frank conversations about what needed to change. There is no doubt that schools face many challenges that can impede performance—budget cuts, teacher shortages, violence—but there are many things within the direct control of educational leaders, such as having and managing high expectations to ensure standards are met. Although it sounds simplistic, many leaders just don't have the necessary critical conversations to reach the goals of the school and the teachers and students who need the most support.

In the end, the schools we led made great strides, met necessary accountability targets, closed achievement gaps, and avoided harsh sanctions. Not only did we make student achievement gains, the school climate was positive. One example is that a few years after Joe became principal in a school that had experienced almost 60 percent teacher turnover, not one teacher left the school. With no teacher positions needing to be filled, the school thrived under the stability. One great achievement T.J. experienced was that after initial resistance from the teachers at the building level, a true working relationship emerged to the point where there was harmony and a total focus on student achievement. This didn't come without a great deal of conflict in either case, but the challenge of leadership is always conflict. It's only when we overcome conflict that we have true influence. With that said, we attribute much of our success to a willingness to tackle tough situations through open and positive communication rooted in candor. Our ultimate discovery is that these conversations are liberating and supportive of change. Both of us have been the disruptor, the person attributed with applying the undesirable pressure to change the system, but through candor we have emerged on the other side of something new and much more effective for a cycle of improving schools within a positive culture.

In addition to our experience in the public school system, we have extensive experience at the post-secondary level as adjunct instructors. In these positions, we continue to hear many of the same issues we faced as building administrators—static levels of achievement, programs not yielding results, high teacher turnover, and overall frustration at both the teacher and administrator levels. The stories and experiences further solidify our belief that many school administrators, despite good intentions, fall short of executing at a high level because they don't use communication as the primary tool to ensure effective implementation of best practices. This book is grounded in our experiences as principals, principal supervisors, and district administrators in two very different settings that faced unique but similar challenges, as well as our findings in leadership development programs that work to support future school leaders.

Candor: The Vehicle for Ensuring Positive Results

In the field of education, we commonly use the phrase "best practice" to indicate something that we universally hold as an improvement strategy—something that, simply put, works in schools and has produced positive results. Reformers and researchers alike use the phrase to mean the same thing—something schools aren't doing that they ought to do or something that schools should keep doing. In fact, Marzano's (2003) highly acclaimed *What Works in Schools* is widely accepted as a "best practices" bible on school leadership among practitioners. Marzano's advice (2003) is organized into "factors," including "implementation," which takes into consideration "the critical role of leadership." This is only one of many publications chocked full of expert advice on strategies to promote change and improvements, most specifically to instruction in the classroom.

Take, for example, another widely accepted instructional leadership publication titled *Leverage Leadership* (Bambrick-Santoyo, 2012). Bambrick-Santoyo (2012) breaks his work into three Parts—"Instruction," "Culture," and "Execution." This work is undeniably practical and takes the frequency of instructional feedback to a new level. Bambrick-Santoyo (2012) made the case that frequent visits to classrooms with scheduled face-to-face meetings with teachers to discuss instruction will make the difference for how students learn in the classroom. We agree, which is one reason we dedicate Part 1 of this book to informal feedback structures.

In 2013, Whitaker, a prolific and accepted educational expert, extended his previous work on "15 Things" to "18 Things That Matter Most" for principals. Included are aspects of leadership like treating everyone with respect and creating a culture of change (Whitaker, 2013). Undoubtedly, these strategies are important "best" practices. What we find is not a flaw in the practices or even practitioners' understanding of the best practices, but rather a gap between knowing and doing. The problem is in the implementation. These practices are studied, learned, and often times even implemented, but not with efficacy.

The challenge is that none of these strategies will work if you simply use them without simultaneously building and developing the right culture. Success in schools is driven by a culture that embraces the big three: informal frequent structures for feedback, a candid communication structure for shared decision-making, and teacher leadership as the backbone. But, all three can be trapped in a circle of nice if the culture isn't one of trust and candor.

Let's meet Jim. Jim is in his third year as the principal of North East High. NE High has a diverse population of over 1100 students, 75 teachers (32 of which have three years' experience or less), and 11 paraprofessionals.

Jim knows the power of walkthroughs and this year decided to visit 10 teachers a week, which is 40 a month. This means that throughout the year he will see each teacher at least four times. Studies in the use of walkthroughs and informal visits to classrooms with subsequent feedback to teachers have demonstrated the positive outcomes on student achievement when the feedback focuses on teachers' use of research-based strategies (Hattie, 2009). Jim is ready and willing to put in the hard work to get the teachers the feedback they need to make changes. However, Jim needs to be careful not to fall into an all-too-common walkthrough trap, which is focusing on getting into the classroom and not necessarily the feedback that the teacher will receive. Walkthroughs possess a unique duality, which is not only what Jim sees during his visit, but how he communicates his feedback to the instructor. The latter part is often overlooked despite its importance for teacher growth. Consider a detective who investigates situations, analyzes the findings, but never reports her conclusions, worse yet, the conclusions are riddled with ambiguity that doesn't represent what the detective actually found.

Despite Jim's efforts he potentially limits his effectiveness and the power of best practice because *being in the classroom* is actually just the beginning. The power lies in what is done with the information collected, which can have many branches—something we discuss later. Too often, though, we become satisfied with simply visiting classrooms with no evidence to show that the walkthroughs are doing anything of instructional value. How does this happen? Actually, it is rather simple. The activity becomes the primary focus and not the desired outcome. Best practices (BPs) are implemented to lead to improved practices and achievement. However, when the activity (best practice) becomes the focal point and not the desired results, key elements to ensure effectiveness are overlooked. To use BPs effectively, the outcomes have to be clear. This is just one example of how a best practice falls short during actual implementation. This pattern of limiting the effectiveness of the best practice due to how it is implemented is not only limited to walkthroughs, but to many "best practices." The implementation of PLCs, the use of distributed leadership models, or even the desire to improve teacher leadership are all diluted as "best practice" without proper execution, and specifically without candor. The primary reason for the lack of candor is a desire to be nice, but we draw a distinction between the two, showing leaders how they can be candid and still be kind without getting trapped in the circle.

Each part of this book addresses a different best practice—informal feedback mechanisms, collaborative decision-making, and teacher leadership—which we consider to be the three biggest levers for driving change in schools. None of these concepts are new, and even though they're proven best practices, touted in the literature, they aren't leveraging the improvements that they could bring about with stronger implementation. Not only is fidelity of implementation critical, BPs must be implemented and supported in a culture of candor. This discussion of candor has somehow not fully made its way into school leadership conversations in the way it has in business (Scott, 2017). However, this powerful communication tool needs to be used alongside each "best practice" for the practice to work. As Jack Welch says, "you have no right to be a leader if someone who works for you doesn't know where they stand" (Goodman, n.d.) And we take this further to include what Simon Sinek calls "starting with why" (2011). If we first communicate the purpose of the best practice, the reason for using it and the intended outcomes, it's far easier to establish the practice within the current culture and even easier to provide people with your most candid and compassionate responses. That's getting outside the circle of nice and that's why we're calling for a candid approach.

The Call for Candor: What It Is and What It Isn't

Organizations can thrive when candor and compassion are part of the fabric for communicating. Prior to delving into what this looks like, we want to clearly outline what it is not. Candor is not being rude, harsh, or simply "honest" or "truthful." Although these things are often associated with candor, in reality, they're much different. A common phrase is, "I'm just being honest," but that's not a preface for honesty, it's a preface for candid speech. For example, honesty delves into virtue and morality while candor is a characteristic of clear communication. In fact, we hope all leaders are honest in their endeavors; however, one can be honest and still not be candid. Replacing the word *honest* with *candor* is important because it diminishes the moral implications of not telling the whole truth (Catmull, 2014). On the other hand, people shy away from being candid because it is often associated with being rude or curt. This sensitivity to being nice is heightened in fields like education where many educators go into the work for altruistic reasons. Our goal is to disassociate candor with rudeness or being unkind and uncover that candor can actually demonstrate a level of care for the individual and the organization. This means that candor isn't honesty or the use of harsh language, but rather an approach to communication that is simply clear and direct and can even create or deepen personal and institutional trust.

Building a culture of candor is intentional. This is because candor is a disposition. Candor is a leadership trait that we contend is critical for organizational success. This also means that it can be learned. Leaders should not only possess this quality, the entire organization must understand the value of candor and use it at all levels. We don't suggest that this is easy, but rather a vital aspect to unearthing the true potential of an organization or individual. However, candor is unfortunately not the norm for most organizations. This is true in both the private and public sectors. In fact, in a study conducted by O'Toole and Bennis, 63 percent of 154 executives surveyed described their company culture as "opaque" (O'Toole & Bennis, 2009). This is not to say that these organizations lack vision but that the organizations in question aren't clear in their communication about their vision, which is often the direct result of trying to be nice.

Despite people shying away from being candid, most people and organizations can benefit from more of it. Imagine a doctor who is not straightforward with someone's diagnosis. Although the diagnosis may not be welcomed, a clear understanding of the ailment is the only way the patient can treat themselves to get well. As such, the vaguer the diagnosis is, the harder it is to treat. This is true for all professions, though, and people are simply not used to operating in an environment where candor is the norm. We contend that leaders can learn to be candid and develop a culture where candor is expected. The value of being candid as an organization is twofold:

1. Being candid as a leader diminishes the natural fear that most people have of conflict. In other words, intentional candor avoids the artificial harmony that comes with a culture of nice by confronting facts and making decisions with them (Lencioni, 2002; Ashkenas, 2010). This means that candor speeds things up. It allows teams to save the time it takes in beating around the bush to getting to a sort of "frankness" as Catmull, President of Pixar and Disney Animation, puts it (2014, p. 86).

2. Candor can actually help to build trust. Many of the researched leadership trust behaviors are about being candid—talk straight, create transparency, confront reality (Covey, 2006). In fact, a lack of candor creates

ambiguity, which can weaken trust and slow things down. This is also where compassionate leadership fits into the equation. When leaders confront issues in an environment of trust, they exhibit compassion, which is our full ability as humans to show kindness and empathy to others.

A culture of real trust requires candor, and communicating with candor demonstrates compassion. Organizations that have deep levels of trust can move quicker than those that don't (Covey, 2006). We're saying that trust is deepened with a candid approach, not the other way around. If your organization lacks candor, you're moving slower than you could if you had it. Using candor builds trust because when everyone knows exactly what everyone else is thinking, no one is making guesses about that. Guessing what people are thinking, especially what the leaders are thinking, slows things down. The last thing we want in schools, or in the use of best practices, is to slow down positive results.

There is also a moral purpose in backing up best practices with candor and communicating outside the circle of nice in schools. Because candor truly does speed up improvements to instruction and subsequent improvements to student learning, not using it is detrimental. We must also consider that using best practices effectively has more of a moral implication in schools than it does on the soccer field or even for the workers at your local hardware store. Not being candid with the use of best practices in schools puts the people in the school, namely the students, at a disadvantage. We contend that there are three big levers in schools—informal feedback to teachers, collaboration and shared decision-making, and teacher leadership. But, these three best practices won't work if you're stuck in the circle of nice. In this book, we'll show you how to use these three practices in the best way possible while communicating outside of the circle of nice, but let's be careful as we move forward.

Be Careful, Candor Can Hurt at First

High expectations that drive toward the mission and goals of the organization have to come with loads of support. If you're working in an environment that doesn't have a candid approach and you decide to be candid tomorrow, be ready to support what you ask people to change. Because candor can hurt at first, it is critical to ensure that the appropriate supports are in place and that the necessary professional development is provided. Consider our principal Jim. He can improve his walkthroughs by giving feedback, but that is only one dimension. The feedback has to be explicit, direct, and supportive. If Jim does this without forewarning, though, his staff won't likely know how to respond. If you're the leader, and you suddenly decide to introduce the *candid effect*, be prepared to explain. Statements like "I'm changing my approach to one that's candid and I expect everyone on this team to do the same" are very important. Candor includes explicitness with our thinking. Not holding anything back, especially when aligned to the vision and mission of the organization, requires the group to recognize, out loud, that we will improve performance through candid and supportive dialogue. The support is critical because acknowledging areas of need and improving performance is only the first step. The goal with candor is to lead to action. Knowledge without action is failure. If Jim decides to introduce the candid feedback after his walkthroughs, he might start each one by saying, "remember, this is the place where we don't hold anything back." It is also necessary to establish norms of trust. So as Jim institutes candid feedback, he also needs to ensure that the staff understands why they need to embrace candor, learn how to be candid, and build support within the environment for the candid approach. This type of out-loud thinking, grounded in cultural norms, can reduce hurt feelings. Taking steps to being outside the circle of nice doesn't mean that we're moving to a culture of mean, but it does need some established groundwork so that it's clear why we're changing our approach.

Establishing a Culture of Trust

The first step in establishing a culture where people are willing to be vulnerable is setting basic norms that outline acceptable behaviors. Norms are often associated with group tasks, but we encourage them to be used in groups, both large and small, as well as in pairs. Norms allow open dialogue. They also create necessary boundaries (such as no personal attacks), limit the dialogue to the topic being discussed, make sure that criticism and praise is specific and constructive, and limit air time. In essence, norms create safety zones for effective communication.

Even so, it takes time to develop a culture of candor in schools. It doesn't take any time for you to be candid, you can do that tomorrow; what takes time is for your candor to be effective and for it to set into the culture. As described, candor may hurt at first, causing setbacks in morale, uneasiness, and even a decrease in communication, which are all things a leader can prepare for and know how to support. Throughout each chapter we will hone in on specific strategies to support best practices through effective implementation nested in a culture of candid communication. We'll show you what a lack of candor looks like and how to fix it with specific words, phrases, and changes to the way we communicate so that you can be candid in your school to maximize the effectiveness of best practices outside the circle of nice.

Getting to Simple: The Structure of Each Part of this Book

We mentioned it before in the Preface, but it's important to note here as you dive into the next sections of this book, that each part is individual and independent of the other parts. You can choose to read this book from cover to cover, but either way we simply suggest that you read this Introduction.

Each part has two chapters to support the best practice. The first chapter in each part begins with the context around the concept, describing how the strategy can be limiting, if not ineffective, if used without a candid approach. We have found that lots of books stop here, admiring the problem without suggesting how to improve it. In the second chapter for each part, we provide specific examples and scenarios to demonstrate what we mean, and we show simple fixes in verbiage and structure that make the approach more candid and much more effective. We also note, where it's relevant, how to sustain the approach when some of the pitfalls occur so that you can push forward even when things don't seem to be improving right away. At the conclusion of each scenario, we provide both a tip for better candid feedback as well as our Candor Cancellations—where we describe a faulty leadership attribute to avoid. These attributes are precisely what leaders do when they're avoiding candid conversations and they create the pitfalls—The What, The Out, and The Blame. The What is a lack of identification in terms of the issues, The Out is the way leaders open the door for a lack of accountability, and The Blame is when we accept excuses for the reasons why things aren't what we expect them to be.

There are three parts to the book. These three parts are actually school improvement strategies and are likely the most written about, studied, heralded, and highly recommended by educational experts. They're also the most fundamental ways in which both of us brought excellence into our schools and districts, which we hope to bring into yours. We hope you find this work to be both invigorating and thoughtful. And we hope that you can use this work to become more candid and more compassionate as a leader.

Informal Teacher Feedback

2 | Blending Instructional Rounds to Guide Walkthroughs

Introduction

In our Preface and Introduction, we set the stage for this book by introducing a candid and compassionate approach to using school and district leadership strategies so that you can step outside the circle of nice. It's imperative that you read both before reading any single chapter of this work. And, as we discussed, you can read each chapter separately as long as you read the Preface and Introduction in their entirety first.

This chapter is dedicated to informal feedback to teachers, specifically through the use of instructional rounds (City, Elmore, Fiarman, Teitel, & Lachman, 2009; Fowler-Fin, 2013; Roberts, 2012; Teitel, 2013) and walkthroughs (Downey, Steffy, English, Frase, & Poston, 2004; Kuchur, Stout, & Edwards, 2013; Moss & Brookhart, 2015). Much has been said about instructional rounds and walkthroughs as a way for both supervisors and peers to visit classrooms to provide informal feedback to teachers to be used to improve practices. The bottom line is that feedback to teachers can improve practice and student achievement, but it has to be done right or it's likely to suffer from being undermined by the receiver (Reeves, 2016).

Generally, as described in the literature available on both topics, instructional rounds are when groups of people (school leaders, teachers, facilitators, etc.) visit classrooms in schools. In other words, they go in and out of classrooms to describe what they see teachers and students doing, particularly how teachers and students are interacting with the content of the lesson (City et al., 2009) and the research-based strategies that teachers are using to engage students (Hattie, 2009). The objective with the rounds is to do informal classroom visits with a number of people and then to debrief about what is happening in the classrooms visited. The proposed result is twofold: 1) teachers and leaders can benchmark, getting on the same page with one another about instructional practices; and 2) they can discuss the kind of feedback that teachers need, based on what they saw, to improve student learning. One of the most important ways to improve candor is to be well-informed and knowledgeable about the practices that we expect to see in classrooms, and rounds offer a way for coaches to engage in discussions that improve their understanding of quality instruction. This happens through both the discussions that ensue and the fact that rounds are inherently led by a facilitator who generally brings either content knowledge of pedagogical expertise to the table.

The walkthrough is quite different in that it is generally described in the literature as an instructional leadership strategy whereby school leaders visit classrooms for a short period of time to provide the teacher with informal feedback. The difference here is that one person, usually the teacher's supervisor or a coach, is providing feedback to the teacher in an informal way, before or after the official observation tool is used for formal evaluation. In the case of rounds, the teachers visited do not get feedback; instead, it's about improving the feedback that we give in subsequent walkthroughs. With walkthroughs, teachers get feedback after each visit.

As such, we contend that instructional rounds should be used to inform walkthroughs. Take, for example, three middle school principals conducting rounds with their curriculum director. In this scenario, the principals and director visit three mathematics classrooms in one school and then discuss the types of questions that the teachers are asking students to evaluate the level of rigor. Let's say that the principals and director conclude that the questioning is at a low recall level and there was opportunity for higher order thinking questions. They should then discuss and decide what kind of feedback would be helpful to the teacher to improve questioning. This is useful for the principals so that they can return to their schools, equipped with feedback they can use when they see questioning at a low level. When this practice of rounds is done often with the very people who do walkthroughs in schools, walkthrough feedback improves. When feedback improves, so can the responses to feedback, which is a change in lesson planning, instructional strategies, and student engagement.

The problem that we address in this chapter is the breakdown within the feedback loop. Too often the information and knowledge gleaned from the rounds remains unused in a practical way. Either principals are using walkthroughs without rounds or principals aren't using walkthroughs at all. Worse yet is that principals may be using walkthroughs, with or without rounds, with less than helpful or productive feedback provided to the teacher because they're trapped in the circle of nice without candor to drive change. Until candid and compassionate feedback is the norm with walkthroughs in schools, not much will change for teaching and learning. We're proposing two things in the following sections:

1. Frequent visits to classrooms

    Supervisors must visit classrooms often in order to provide quality and effective feedback to teachers. In other words, when teachers are only visited once, twice, or three times a year, as a result of singular and isolated visits, the feedback is disjointed and cannot effectively capture their scope of work and their impact on students in their classrooms. Quality feedback begins with frequent visits to classrooms, which then, and only then, enables the administrator to know and understand the breadth and depth of what is being taught and how well students are being instructed. This may be a simple notion, but the fact remains that large numbers of teachers report not being visited frequently for the purpose of coaching in cycles of improvement.

2. Quality feedback loops

    Frequent visits to the classroom is just the beginning. Quality and effective feedback is critical to teacher improvement and student achievement. When supervisors are visiting classrooms frequently but only providing minimal or poor feedback to teachers, the best practice of conducting walkthroughs is lost and becomes altogether ineffective. Feedback might be poor for a number of reasons, but we contend that it's mostly due to a lack of candor and not due to a lack of professional aptitude. Supervisors often fail to say what they think in a candid manner during informal classroom visits and during instructional rounds. As a result, walkthroughs and rounds have little impact on instruction.

Without helpful and meaningful feedback to teachers, spending time in classrooms only promotes presence, which isn't enough to improve practice. This keeps us within our comfort zone or what we call *the circle of nice*, and it thwarts any real change. Simply getting into the classroom can create an illusion of effectiveness, which can mask whether or not the rounds and walkthroughs are having positive outcomes. The desire to grow as professionals must drive our desire to fully utilize the best practice of informal feedback, and it takes candor and compassion to realize the effectiveness of their use in schools.

Using Instructional Rounds and Walkthroughs

Fowler-Fin (2013) described instructional rounds as "helping us figure out and describe what good teaching and learning look like, [which] helps us uncover ways that we can support each other to get there." We take this one step further to say that instructional rounds should be used to inform subsequent walkthrough feedback. This strategy of using rounds to inform feedback is not new and it's not unique to education. The medical field has been using rounds for years to inform practice, collaborate on decisions, and use that collaboration for learning what to say and do in subsequent visits to patients. The process is exactly the same in education, or at least should be. Doctors inform their individual feedback to patients by using rounds to learn more about diagnosing and curing illness. Educational leaders can inform their feedback in walkthroughs by doing rounds with other leaders who wish to improve their instructional focus.

The problem is that with all that has been said about doing instructional rounds in schools, they're still rare and infrequent. This means that principals who do walkthroughs are doing so without any other structure to inform what they're saying to teachers when they visit classrooms. Without rounds, all of the responsibility for quality feedback is left to the principal. We're not saying that principals shouldn't assume all responsibility for their schools. We are saying that relying on one individual (with the help of assistant principals) to define what teachers read and hear as feedback on their lessons is irresponsible to the point of being farfetched in even working. Of course, many school principals are capable of being thorough and thoughtful in their response to classroom visits. But to never or infrequently discuss these visits with other instructional leaders creates a vacuum of feedback rather than feedback that could be informed by the perspectives and expertise of others. It also means that we're likely to move more toward the center of the circle of nice than the edges where candor lives. The reason is that in the vacuum, without rounds, the feedback will likely be given through the lens of someone who sees people far more subjectively than would be the case if we collaborated about what we see in classrooms.

In other words, without rounds, the principal's perspective is limited. We tout collaboration among students within in the classroom as a 21st- century skill, yet fail to systematically practice it as a profession. As a result, the principal's experience is only informed by the individual walkthroughs that she does and not structured conversations with other leaders regarding what we see holistically in a principal's school and elsewhere in the district and beyond. When principals aren't equipped with a consensus for the vision and direction of instruction in their school, their work becomes marginalized through an insulated approach. What they say to teachers may be shallow, less than constructive, or even incorrect. Furthermore, when we consider the ever-changing and growing list of responsibilities heaped on principals, developing an infrastructure to support principals that combines walkthroughs with the power of instructional rounds is critical.

Fullan (2014) tells readers that "principals' responsibilities have increased enormously over the past two decades," and yet the job has become lonelier than ever and almost "impossible" (p. 6). His book, *The Principal*, describes a shift whereby the principal is the chief instructional leader but is supported by other instructional leaders in the school (Fullan, 2014). We're saying that instructional rounds are one support for principals to be more effective at providing focused feedback during walkthroughs. And, the rounds provide a time for more than just the principal to visit classrooms and collaborate on what we should be saying to teachers subsequent to the rounds themselves. This approach goes beyond the principal as the sole owner of the instructional leadership paradigm and includes any school or district leader invited to participate in the rounds and the discussion about how to push the boundaries of instructional practices to a new level. The key is the conversation and the efforts to get better at giving feedback, and that's the cross-section of knowing what to say and knowing how to say it in a candid and compassionate way so that the actual improvements are made.

Let's revisit our principal Jim. As an example, let's say that a curriculum director, Jim, and two other high school principals visit all of the mathematics classrooms at the 10th grade level in all three schools over the course of a day and a half. The focus of the rounds can be to look for what the teacher is doing, what the students are doing, and what the learning task is at the time of the visit (City et al., 2014). The objective is to see if the lessons' essential questions, which the curriculum department worked on a year ago, are still in place, consistently taught in sequence, and that students are collaborating (a structure that all three principals have provided PD for in the last year or two). Let's say the findings are that two of the three schools are teaching the same EQs but the third school, which is Jim's, has deviated from the curriculum-developed essential questions and that mostly the visits show teachers providing direct instruction. In other words, collaborative structures, even after two years of PD, are not the norm.

These findings, from instructional rounds, prove informative for the three principals in their subsequent walkthroughs. However, Jim must start to provide very direct feedback around the use of EQs and district sequencing, likely something that he wouldn't have caught doing walkthroughs on his own. All three principals need to be providing very direct feedback regarding the use of strategies that they know their teachers have learned in PD and should be using. Maybe this is something that any individual principal would have discovered on his own, but here we can collaborate on the types of things that we expect in the district and the types of direction we can provide teachers in our walkthrough feedback. Working with the curriculum director, we might even devise a coaching plan for working with our mathematics teachers on collaborative structures in the classroom. Often, PD is not enough for practices to stick. Teachers need further support through direct walkthrough feedback and push-in coaches to help with planning and even real-time instructional delivery. None of this can be identified without instructional rounds. Let's consider this cycle of feedback using the following model as a simple process.

The First Round of Rounds

During the first round of instructional rounds, leaders from across the school system would come together to make classroom visits in teams. The teams have a focus. In the previously mentioned focus, the leaders are looking at curriculum mapping and pacing of the content across middle schools along with instructional strategies that teachers recently learned how to use. Let's take the example of the curriculum maps for our modeled cycle. When Jim realizes that his teachers have deviated from the maps, he is now informed of what he needs to do with his feedback to teachers in the coming weeks and months. He needs to get them back on track by asking direct questions and providing support when needed.

School-Based Walkthroughs

For the purpose of the cycle, after the rounds, leaders go back to doing daily walkthroughs with feedback to teachers. In the case of Jim, he's now asking questions about the curriculum pacing to include his findings from the other schools. He can say with confidence that the maps show that the teachers should be using certain questions that they're not, and he can ask his teachers why that is. He may even need to say, please don't use that question but rather the ones that can be found in our district's curriculum, and invite his teachers to discuss their rationale for changing the question but with the notion that while the district encourages input from teachers, they don't have the authority to change the curriculum on their own. Notice that it's the rounds that uncovered the problem and improved the depth of Jim's feedback about teaching practices in his schools. The model doesn't stop there; more rounds are needed.

The Second Round of Rounds

As the example continues, the team goes back to all three middle schools for more rounds, a second round of rounds. They are again looking for curriculum pacing and instructional strategies as their focus. Let's say that in this round the leaders find that Jim has clearly gotten his teachers back on track with pacing. They're using the district maps and essential questions, and all three schools are up to speed with their units, only days apart in delivery of what DuFour and Marzano (2011) call a guaranteed and viable curriculum. The new problem for Jim is that his teachers are still behind with the collaborative structures. They're back on track with the maps but direct instruction is still the norm. Jim might be pleased with his progress, but he has work to do. His focus was on the curriculum mapping, and now he needs to support his teachers' usage of new strategies.

School-Based Walkthroughs

In the cycle, Jim is now back at school, conducting walkthroughs with feedback to teachers. His focus is on the use of collaborative structures that the teachers have been trained to use. With the right feedback, there's no doubt that Jim can change classroom practices. He's been informed and empowered by the use of instructional rounds, whereby his focus becomes clear through collaboration with other leaders on the same mission to provide quality classroom experiences for students. As with most teachers, given an opportunity for feedback and dialogue, things are bound to move in the right direction, but if Jim lacks candor in his feedback or compassion for his people when he delivers it, nothing is likely to change at all.

Thus, doing walkthroughs, without informing them with rounds, leads to a lack of focused commentary for teachers, which leads to a lack of candor in walkthrough feedback. The result is very little, if any, change to instructional practices, even if the leader is visiting classrooms and providing feedback. Reeves (2009) reminds readers that "any change will meet resistance" in schools (p. 45). We can overcome resistance to change with a consistent message. Going from room to room, providing feedback to teachers, but with an inconsistent uninformed message is not only ineffective, it can lead teachers to devalue the walkthrough process and the feedback. The challenge is ensuring that we are maximizing our efforts and utilizing our precious time most effectively. This is not only limited to the quality of the feedback, but how skillfully it is delivered. Candor, then, must be the engine driving the feedback and compassionate leadership is at its core.

Instructional Leadership: Candid Feedback

One major problem with walkthroughs in education is the difficulty with providing quality feedback to teachers due to the fact that during the visit, the teacher is teaching. Conducting walkthroughs in schools stems from a management strategy that was introduced in 1982 by Thomas Peters and Robert Waterman in their book, *In Search of Excellence*. The strategy, then called Management by Walking Around, held the simple philosophy that interactions between managers and staff can improve practices (Peters & Waterman, 1982). In other words, frequent feedback to workers because the manager is on the frontlines, in the important production space, refines and enhances business operations. Fast forward more than a decade, and like many business strategies that don't quite translate to educational reform, walkthroughs arrive on the scene as an instructional leadership best practice. The intentions are well-centered, the theory is solid, but visiting the most important spaces in schools doesn't equal quality, in-the-moment feedback to teachers.

The biggest problem with using this practice in education is that providing teachers with dynamic real-time *verbal* feedback while they're teaching is almost impossible. This leaves the school leader with a feedback mechanism that is likely *written*. Walkthrough feedback tools come in the form of written notes, online or written forms, or email. This poses a problem because written feedback often comes with unintended tone and is void of the critical dialogue necessary in improving one's performance. As such, when the leader provides written feedback, it is subjected to the culture of nice, whereby nothing really substantive is said for fear that the teacher will misinterpret the meaning and become offended when that was never the intention. This means that leaders are likely to hold back from giving direct feedback for fear that the feedback won't be interpreted accurately, and thus, the feedback becomes ambiguous and less than useful. The brain research on giving feedback supports this notion in that it's often the case that feedback providers revert to a flight-or-fight mechanism in the brain, preventing them from providing feedback due to the fear that they'll hurt the receiver's feelings (Carrol, 2014). Albeit the case that feedback is not always welcomed, it is a necessary function for improving practice (Douglas & Sheila, 2014), not to mention the fact that the more feedback we give the better we get at it, and the more feedback we receive the better we respond to it.

In their review of successful companies, including Disney, Hewlett-Packard, and Walmart, Peters and Waterman (1982) contended that management's interactions with workers allowed managers to understand worker job satisfaction and job-related frustrations that the manager might address in the moment as well as to provide needed feedback to improve worker effectiveness in quick face-to-face conversations. Another byproduct of this type of feedback is a culture where managers and workers are together in the most important space in their organization, making decisions that affect productivity in a positive way. Educators can't implement this practice without giving serious thought to what it means to interact during walkthroughs and what it means to provide feedback to teachers that can do what Peters and Waterman (1982) proposed in their work. If we're searching for excellence in schools, we need to be candid about what we think is excellent and what we know is not. The problem is that most feedback is not candid enough to make a difference and leaders need practice to ensure that candor is received through a compassionate approach.

The clearest example of candid and compassionate feedback in rounds and walkthroughs comes from Pixar in a time when Ed Catmull and

Steve Jobs were building an empire, preparing to release animated films in a way that had never been done before. Catmull (2014) described doing "rounds" with Jobs. The rounds they conducted were meant to inform them as leaders in terms of what they needed to do to improve the company, specifically to improve the culture of creativity. Catmull also described these rounds as a place for candid conversations between him and Jobs and often between Jobs and other Pixar employees. This candid approach to providing feedback happened during their rounds and also in the feedback that they gave filmmakers on their iterations of soon-to-be features. The level of candor described by Catmull in his book *Creativity, Inc.* demonstrates a commitment to excellence but also the understanding that change can only come from very honest and direct sources. Catmull and his team created the "Braintrust" as a candor-centered think-tank to review creative projects. He says that "people who take on complicated creative projects become lost at some point in the process." It is for this precise reason that people need candid feedback. They become lost in their projects, protective of their ideas, and can't see the truth. In a culture where candor is the norm, Pixar broke through the outer rim of the circle of nice so that their product was more than one person's or a small team's insulated enterprise.

This is the type of culture that schools need for instructional rounds and walkthroughs. Leading a school or teaching a class is a creative project where Catmull would say there's a real need for candor because "fears and instincts for self-preservation often cause us to hold back" (p. 87). Holding back doesn't help teachers to grow and doesn't help students to learn. Instead we need rounds to inform our feedback and feedback to be candid and focused. Only then will our cultures of excellence flourish outside the circle of nice, which has many more benefits to the people in our organizations than just stronger feedback for performance purposes.

Using walkthroughs in schools as an instructional leadership strategy can do more than just improve classroom instruction. In fact, more than ten years ago, Downey et al. (2004) claimed that walkthroughs can aid with teacher job satisfaction, teacher self-efficacy, post-lesson reflection, and more. That is assuming that the teacher is getting feedback after the walkthrough that actually prompts a thoughtful response. And that assumes that the teacher is getting feedback at all. In 2008, Skretta found that feedback to teachers subsequent to walkthroughs was an inconsistent practice. We would like to think that almost a decade later feedback after short visits to classrooms would be the norm, but you have to determine if that's the case in your school or district, or not.

Figure 2.1 Feedback Cycle

For the purpose of our discussion regarding walkthroughs, we assume that every walkthrough visit to classrooms comes with feedback to the teacher. Furthermore, visiting classrooms without giving feedback, unless the teacher knows that there's a different purpose (as in the case of instructional rounds), can prove to be problematic. To enter a classroom, especially as the principal of the school or the teacher's supervisor, and then to say nothing to the teacher about what we saw creates uncertainty. We take this one step further to say that a lot of the time when feedback *is* given it's ineffective. The feedback needs to be specific, constructive, and candid to make a difference for the teacher. We're not necessarily saying that this is due to the leader's inability to say something constructive. We are saying that the leader is typically holding something back for fear that she will offend the teacher. The problem is that holding back our thoughts, because we don't want to offend, is likely to do exactly that, offend the teacher. Offending teachers in schools will not do what the walkthrough strategy is proposed to do—improve practices, decrease burnout, increase self-efficacy, and prompt reflection (Downey et al., 2004). We're saying that we can fix that by being candid and compassionate with frequent visits to classrooms with quality feedback to teachers. Nothing will do more for the profession than growing our teachers' capacity to deliver impactful experiences for students, and every teacher deserves a coach. Next, we dive into specific examples of what we mean by this and simple fixes that will be easy to implement (Figure 2.1).

Candid and Compassionate Feedback that Works

Examples to Guide Practice

Introduction

The following are three examples of walkthrough feedback that can be improved with candor. We'll point out when the observer is being offensive and how to fix that with more direct and actionable advice to the teacher. For each example, we'll describe what the observer actually saw and what she thought when she visited the room. We'll then describe what was said to the teacher and how that is often different from what the leader saw and thought. We'll then show how simple fixes can make a difference, how being more candid can actually prevent offensiveness.

Scenario One

Classroom Walkthrough

Principal: Mrs. Lewis
    Teacher: Mrs. Jacobs
    Class: 7th period English, 10th grade
    Demographics:

- 27 students
  - 15 females, 12 males
- Inclusive class
  - Six special education

What the Observer Saw

It was 7th period English, Mrs. Jacobs' room. Mrs. Jacobs is in her sixth year teaching 10th grade English and the class was reading *Things Fall Apart* by Chinua Achebe. I was first struck by the incredible bulletin board displaying aspects of the book and Nigerian tribal culture. At first glance, it appeared that all students were engaged—books were on their desk and they appeared to be following along while Mrs. Jacobs read a part of the book. The students even had a *Things Fall Apart* graphic organizer next to them. Once Mrs. Jacobs was done reading, she called on Brittany who began to read for a time and then once she completed a portion, John was called on to read. This process continued, and for those ten minutes, six different students read. Each of the students read after the other and were called on by Mrs. Jacobs.

What the Observer Thought

The best way to describe what was seen in Mrs. Jacobs' room in today's walkthrough was missed opportunities. It was obvious Mrs. Jacobs spent a great deal of time preparing the students to read *Things Fall Apart*. The stage was set with an informative bulletin board, the graphic organizer was designed for students to interact with the text and grapple with ideas; however, the instructional strategy fell short. Mrs. Jacobs decided to use Round Robin Reading and not a current research-based instructional strategy that ensures student engagement to reinforce comprehension and fluency. There are various strategies that can be used and if the teacher wants to listen to the students read aloud, strategies such as paired reading and choral reading are much more effective (Sharpe, 2009).

What the Observer Actually Said in the Feedback to the Teacher

Mrs. Jacobs,

Setting the stage and providing the correct context for any reading is important. I liked the detailed bulletin board; it was impressive!

(Continued)

Regarding student engagement, it appeared students were following along while others were reading out loud. You used Round Robin Reading (RRR) as the reading strategy and during that time six of your twenty-seven students read out loud. I'm curious as to how many students read out loud and if RRR is a consistent strategy that you use? Lastly, I noticed that the students had a graphic organizer, which can be a powerful tool.

What Should Have Been Different

The original lesson observed during the walkthrough has key elements of an effective lesson. Any observer could have easily walked out of Mrs. Jacobs' room thinking this was an effective lesson and not offer any suggestions to improve practice. Why? The teacher was prepared and her lesson was well planned to include a striking bulletin board. In addition, the students appeared to be engaged, well behaved, and seemingly following along. The difference, though, is that the instructional strategy is questionable and the graphic organizer wasn't used. Depending on the student makeup of the classroom, such as the special education students, RRR could potentially limit and possibly adversely affect fluency and comprehension development, maybe even prompt an embarrassing situation for a student. An alternative literacy strategy would have allowed students to read, but also minimized their vulnerability to a room full of other novice readers. The teacher needs to know that readers should be grouped in smaller groups or given an opportunity to listen to how the passage should be read from an "expert" reader (Finley, 2014). Lastly, requiring students to engage and interact with the text through the use of the graphic organizer would have enhanced the lesson and their learning. The structure of the lesson didn't allow for students to stop and think about what they were reading.

How to Fix the Feedback

The following are simple questions and sentence stems to utilize either in writing or while engaging in a face-to-face meeting. Or, what we like to refer to as a knee-to-knee conversation. We utilize questions simply for the teacher to reflect on her own practice and to create dialogue. Too often the "telling" or "suggesting" on the observer's part falls short of actually changing practice. Too much "telling" can limit the reflection that questions might prompt. But, be careful that the questions are genuine. In this scenario, there are questions to ask and other more direct statements to make that should not be phrased as questions.

Questions to Ask

- How much of the book is read in class?
- How do you know the students who are not reading were engaged?
- How do you ensure students are interacting with the text?
- How are you extending students' thinking with questions after they read?

These questions are "genuine" because they speak to the flaw of a walk-through, which is that the observer is only in the room to see a limited portion of a much more complex lesson. These questions offer the teacher a prompt to reflect on the usage of in-class time, student engagement while reading, student-to-text interactions, and some of what the observer can't see in a short time, which is how students move to higher order thinking after they read. But, there are also questions not to ask.

Questions Not to Ask

- What changes would you make?
- Why did you choose RRR?

We argue that these questions are limiting. They might be the normal knee-jerk responses from an observer who wants to talk about changing this lesson, but they assume that the teacher wants to make changes too and that the teacher chose RRR from some bank of strategies she has. If the observer doesn't want to see RRR for any well-researched reason, then she should just say so rather than asking questions about it. Questions should not be asked in a passive way to ultimately get to the observer's point. This is disingenuous and will create animosity. Rather, questions are designed to create dialogue, dig deeper into how the lesson was planned and why strategies were chosen. If the observer believes that RRR is ineffective then that should simply be said with sufficient reason.

Stems to Help Guide Your Feedback that Are More Direct and Offer Improved Alternatives

- Reading aloud to your students has several benefits, one being an improved classroom environment, while allowing you to model "expert" reading. Research supports students listening to a text the way it is supposed to be read. Have you considered bringing in an audio version? That might improve the quality of what they hear as the read along in the text.

- RRR, although popular, has more drawbacks than advantages. If you want to listen to students read, paired reading is a superior alternative. If you want to work on fluency and comprehension, choral reading is a better choice. RRR causes too much vulnerability for kids who struggle to read and can frustrate those who want to read faster in their heads. Try using something different next time and let me know how it works.

- The graphic organizer was well developed and should be infused into the reading. Having students grapple with ideas and interact with the text will increase comprehension. I saw that you had the graphic organizer prepared, but I didn't see how they were supposed to engage with it during the reading activity. Research supports *before, during*, and *after* reading strategies. Nice job having a graphic organizer available for *during* reading, but be sure that they are using and interacting with the tool.

Notice that all three bullets address the problems observed with simple fixes. Students need to hear good reading, the teacher should not be using RRR, and the graphic organizer needed to be in use during the reading activity. Instead of being "curious" about RRR, the observer should be direct in that it's not effective. Instead of "noticing" the graphic organizer, the observer needed to ask the teacher to have it be more prevalent in the activity for it to be effective. Let's take a look at what the observer could have said.

What the Observer Could Have Said with Candor

Mrs. Jacobs,

Setting the stage for any reading is important. During the walk-through it appeared that students were following along and reading aloud. However, Round Robin Reading can have three unintended negative consequences. One, it limits engagement by students potentially zoning out while others read. Two, it may negatively affect fluency and reading comprehension if certain students cannot read well. Three, certain students may feel embarrassed and create a difficult situation where the student refuses to read and feels ashamed by their reading ability.

If you want to listen to students as they read, partner reading is very effective. If you are interested in their fluency and comprehension, choral reading is a good alternative. Also, embedding the graphic organizer into the assignment while they're reading will enhance their interaction with the text and create an improved learning situation. The graphic organizer is well developed and can be a powerful tool. The elements of a great lesson are present; the key is simply organizing them to maximize their effectiveness.

Lastly, the detailed bulletin board was impressive! The visuals were powerful and helped the students connect with the book and the material.

I appreciated being here today. My door is always open if you want to discuss.

Notice that the improved feedback is much more direct. It now has the power to change practice instead of leaving the teacher with more questions than answers. It's direct, rather than simply being nice, whereby holding back candid feedback and just writing a narrative of what was observed wouldn't be helpful or likely to improve anything based on the visit. Notice, too, that there are simply more thoughts shared. Really short feedback has the potential to be interpreted as less than the full story and even unimportant. Both are offensive byproducts of informal feedback gone wrong due to an observer's desire to be nice.

Here's a Tip

Use data, visit often.
One critical point to consider is that the walkthrough feedback can be dismissed by teachers if they feel the observer doesn't know the dynamics of their class. The easiest way to avoid this criticism is to learn about the class. Quick data digs to learn about the students can increase your awareness of the makeup of the students, which allows you to offer even greater detailed feedback for the teacher. We should also note, again, that walkthroughs don't work unless they are frequent. You can increase the value of your feedback by visiting teachers often, simply by the fact that your walkthroughs will be more informed by environmental factors that you can only pick up on over time.

Candor Cancellation #1—*The Holder Backer*

Don't be someone who thinks something but doesn't say it. Leaders can't hold back, and candor requires open sharing of thoughts and ideas. Mrs. Lewis knew that the reading strategy was ineffective, and instead of giving direct feedback for a needed change, she asked a question about it. She holds back her thoughts, and it cancels any candid conversation that could follow. It's far better to be aggressive with direct feedback than it is to be passive aggressive through questioning.

Scenario Two

Classroom Walkthrough

Principal: Mr. Lee
 Teacher: Mr. Barnes
 Class: 2nd period Social Studies, 7th grade
 Demographics:
- 25 students
  - 12 females, 13 males

What the Observer Saw

Mr. Barnes teaches 7th grade Social Studies and he is in his fifth year of teaching. As Mr. Lee entered the classroom, the students, 25 in all, were returning to their seats, notebooks in hand, after what appeared to be a gallery walk. Throughout the room, there were seven stations that had some type of information on the topic. Mr. Lee was able to note that one station had images of revolutions, another had a video for students to watch, and a third had some writing pieces. As the students returned to their seats, Mr. Lee was excited to hear the follow-up conversations. Mr. Barnes assigned each group a station to report out their findings and then called on each group to identify their most important finding. While each group reported out, the other groups were directed to write down the main points. At one point, Mr. Barnes even made reference to the Essential Question. After each group went, Mr. Barnes filled in specific details for each area, and when the reports were all finished, he proceeded to show a video.

What the Observer Thought

Mr. Barnes was a recent hire, new to the school and his previous experiences and skill set are clearly making a positive impact on the 7th grade team. He is energetic and full of good ideas. Regarding the lesson, Mr. Lee was glad to see the various stations and how the lesson had differentiated sources at each. What Mr. Lee couldn't shake was Howard Gardner's theory that coverage is the enemy of understanding (Gardner, 1991). Mr. Barnes fell victim to the common trap of trying to cover a great deal of information through the use of a good instructional strategy. It was evident that Mr. Barnes planned well and ensured that the stations for the gallery walk had relevant and detailed information. The information was aligned to the standards and the essential question reflected the information being taught. It was even great to hear Mr. Lee refer back to the Essential Question. The challenge was that the students were simply gathering information either from the station, each other, or the teacher. The students were not extending their thinking, nor were they analyzing or problem solving. One fundamental mistake was that the activity didn't require the students to interact with each other, the content at each station, or through the debrief. The lesson was well planned with the content, but the instructional piece fell short whereby students were retrieving information rather than analyzing it. The gallery walk is intended to expose students to a few concepts for a deeper dig, but it's all too often used for covering content rather than digging into it in a station-like format. The challenge with giving feedback to Mr. Barnes is in providing instructional advice and recommendations that make this lesson effective, while at the same time communicating that Mr. Barnes knows how much of an asset he is to the team and to the school. He had a good plan but it won't get students to think more than at the surface level.

What the Observer Actually Said in the Feedback to the Teacher

Mr. Barnes,

Using galleries walks as an instructional strategy to create discussions while utilizing a variety of sources is an effective instructional strategy. The preparation of materials and stations for the lesson was evident, students had notebooks in hand, and the groups called on were able to cite specific information from each station. I would consider developing ways to increase student interaction with one another and the content. I also noticed how you referenced the EQ during the one group's report out. Nice job!

I look forward to seeing your class again!

What Should have Been Different

Mr. Barnes' lesson was well planned and had elements to be very effective. The challenge was that in his attempt to try to "cover" information and simply have students record information, student learning was limited and the instructional activity was compromised. The goal is to help Mr. Barnes understand that this lesson, with some minor tweaks, can be very effective. The key is to communicate a message that recognizes the strengths of the lesson and how it can be improved, but the challenge is in moving from being "nice" to being candid. Teachers want to grow as professionals and many, similar to Mr. Barnes, have good lessons that can become great. In this instance, the observer shies away from critical feedback since the lesson has good qualities, and because Mr. Barnes is a new hire who is doing well. Too often, administrators fear that feedback will be perceived negatively, and rather than creating dialogue, the fear is that the feedback will actually cause the teacher to shut down. The unfortunate result is that Mr. Lee ended up being nice rather than being helpful. The mistake is easily fixed by using a combination of very direct feedback about what needs to be improved while providing specific praise on the elements of the plan that were effective. For example, a simple suggestion to create a worksheet with prompts versus allowing students to take notes in their notebook would improve rigor. This simple step could enable the teacher to engage the students at each station and tailor what he wants them to focus on. Not only will this guide the students and their conversations, depending on the type of questions on the sheet, it can also be collected and used in a variety of different ways. Mr. Barnes asks students to collect information, but specific questions about the content embedded in a graphic organizer could take this gallery walk to a new level. The principal knows that, but that's not what he said in his feedback. Again, we sacrifice our improvement efforts to stay in the circle of nice.

How to Fix the Feedback

A gallery walk is designed to create discussion; however, Mr. Barnes used it as a method to disseminate information. The following more direct feedback to Mr. Barnes could have been used to prompt reflection from the teacher and demonstrate something new for him to think about as he plans his next gallery walk.

Examples of More Direct Feedback

- Mr. Barnes, rather than allowing students to write key ideas in a notebook, create a worksheet that engages each student with the content and one another at each station. Probing questions that extend their thinking beyond obtaining the basic concepts will enrich their learning experience.

- During the debrief, create discussions that move beyond the knowledge level. Having students tie the information to previously learned content and getting them to create new ideas is paramount.

- Mr. Barnes, I think I understand that you're trying to use the gallery walk as a strategy to cover the content that you linked to the LEQ. That's a great first step. Try using a graphic organizer for each station that includes specific questions that take students beyond recall and retrieval and further up the Cognitive Growth Targets (Smith, Chavez, & Seaman, 2016) that we've discussed at our faculty meetings.

Note that the feedback is direct and doesn't leave room for any ambiguity through being nice with words but saying what you really mean. The first bullet provides replacement language, like "rather than," which prompts the teacher to replace a strategy with another. The second bullet isn't a suggestion, the supervisor is saying "create discussions that move beyond..." Although the feedback is informal, it isn't optional for the teacher to make improvements based on it. The third bullet is an example where the observer can make mention of something good that might be the first step for something that could be great. Too often, teachers spend time on low-level questioning and need to move on to higher order thinking questions. It's also critical to refer back to any professional development that is ongoing and expected to make changes in the classroom. Let's see what some of this looks like in action.

What the Observer Could Have Said with Candor

Mr. Barnes,

Using gallery walks as an instructional strategy to create discussions while utilizing a variety of sources is an effective instructional strategy. The preparation for the lesson was evident with the various resources at each station. Overall, the observed portion of this lesson had very sound qualities. So much was in place, and I believe that with some minor adjustments you will unveil the full potential of your preparation and the instructional strategy.

In order to enhance the lesson and get the most from gallery walks, I suggest the following:

1. Create a worksheet ahead of time that prompts the students at each station and focuses their attention. The prompts can vary. For example, after students identify key ideas, have them also identify what resonates with them, what they find challenging, or even how the information ties into previously learned material.

In addition, you can have them, within their "team," draw connections to real-world applications and also create questions they have during the visit to each station.

2. Gallery walks are great at creating collaboration and you want to ensure that you achieve this through the activities that you create. Consider less stations, more dialogue, and enhancing the whole class debrief by allowing them to ask the questions they created. Once they have the basic concepts, it is critical to find ways to extend their thinking (Gallery Walk, n.d.).

I think you're a great addition to the team and our school, and I look forward to seeing you and your class in action again.

Here the observer is far more direct, getting outside the circle of nice, and moving to a real improvement strategy with informal feedback. We contend that all the feedback in the world won't change anything unless it is direct, specific, and actionable. The observer is direct with both praise and the needed adjustments to the lesson, and Mr. Barnes can make no mistake in reading this that he has a good lesson, which needs tweaks to better support learning, and his place on the team and in the school is one of importance to the principal.

Here's a Tip

Number your suggestions.
The principal had two key thoughts—that the students need a stronger structure for collaborating and that the teacher needed better learning prompts and a graphic organizer. In the second more direct feedback example, both thoughts were clear. When you think about one or two things that can improve a lesson, focus on those two things and be clear. In fact, clarity through enumeration is important, especially if you plan to revisit the feedback whereby the numbering allows both you and the teacher to recall the suggestions faster than reading through prose. And, teachers can easily respond to very specific advice, especially when it's only one or two things to change. Too often, we ask teachers to change too much or we're too vague about what we're asking them to change.

Candor Cancellation #2—*The Ambiguoust*

Don't be ambiguous with your words. It's not helpful. It's better to be direct than to be flowery, and that goes for both praise and corrective feedback. The teacher can't grow if she doesn't know what you mean or you simply don't say what you mean. The Ambiguoust gives themselves and the teacher an out with a message that's so unclear it's impossible to take action based on it. Being ambiguous cancels candor completely.

Scenario Three

Classroom Walkthrough

Principal: Mr. Ames
Teacher: Mrs. Smith
Class: 1st grade
Demographics:

- 22 students
  - 12 females, 10 males

- 3 special education
  - 2 English learners

What the Observer Saw

Mrs. Smith teaches 1st grade and is in her 11th year of teaching. When Mr. Ames entered the classroom, the students were wrapping up a spelling lesson, utilizing *Words Their Way*. As the students put their items away, they transitioned from their desks to the carpet for a writing mini-lesson. During the transition, some students followed the directions quietly, orderly, and quickly, some lingered around their desks, and a few ran to the carpet, and rather than sitting down, they simply fell or jumped into place. To regain control, Mrs. Smith called out to the students who weren't complying and had to repeat the directions twice more. Once the students were seated, a few minutes later, they started the mini lesson, which was on how to write directions and the use of sequential words. Mrs. Smith had the Smartboard divided into two halves and had nine boxes with pictures depicting the steps on how to brush your teeth. In each box, there was an "order word" and she led a discussion on the order boxes. Mrs. Smith demonstrated the steps for the students to work on writing their own directions for something other than teeth brushing.

What the Observer Thought

Mr. Ames was impressed with the writing lesson, the level of modeling, and the use of the Smartboard. However, the transition he observed was ineffective. Several minutes were wasted during the move to the carpet and Mrs. Smith, even if only for a couple seconds, lost control. In fact, Mr. Ames was a little surprised by the level of the instructional activity as compared to the poor transition. Mr. Ames somehow thought that Mrs. Smith, who plans for great instruction, would also have good management and timing, but that's not the case. It was such a glaring issue because she is using good strategies in one moment and then losing control of the students in the next.

What the Observer Actually Said in the Feedback to the Teacher

Mrs. Smith,

The mini-lesson on the writing piece was well developed. The modeling and examples, which were organized and displayed visually on the Smartboard, were excellent. Your instructional organization prevented unnecessary questions and the students understood the lesson. It was also great to see the effective use of the Smartboard, whereby you used the two-halves feature. I don't always see the boards being used with all their bells and whistles. Please work on transitioning to the carpet with less disruption.

What Should have Been Different

In this instance, Mr. Ames clearly wanted to identify and praise the instructional components of the lesson, but he glosses over the rocky transition. There is no doubt that the mini-lesson was well organized, reinforced through modeling, and supported and enhanced through the Smartboard. However, that is why it is critical to view a lesson through multiple lenses—planning and preparation, classroom environment, and instruction. In this instance, the classroom management aspect of the lesson must be addressed, despite the instructional success. While Mr. Ames is bold enough to say "please work on transitioning to the carpet with less disruption" and we support this as a first layer of candor, it still doesn't help the teacher to improve practices through specific and candid suggestions. Mr. Ames could have noted the disparity between instructional practice and management, and "work on" is ambiguous. Mr. Ames needs to note exactly what happened as evidence and then support Mrs. Smith with specific suggestions for improvement. Just saying "work on" implies that Mrs. Smith isn't good at it, which may leave her offended. Providing evidence to support the need to "work on" and then suggestions for improvement is more candid, provides clarity for the teacher, and gives the teacher something to actually "work on."

How to Fix the Feedback

Praising the instructional aspect of the lesson and clearly identifying the effective components is paramount. Duplicating best practices is critical to mastery teaching. However, one good part of a lesson shouldn't negate constructive criticism of another. Too often, observers want to praise teachers without providing any details for how to improve a lesson. Whitaker (2013) reminds principals to do for everyone what they would do for their best teachers. Our best teachers want critical feedback. Another important aspect of feedback is that it's super specific. Our example in this case is the observer saying "work on" when we don't really know what that means. It's no different than telling teachers to improve student engagement without actually defining what it looks like for students to be engaged.

The following conversation starters can help prompt a conversation to reinforce best practices and may help with classroom management techniques for Mrs. Smith. We also include questions not to ask, which are bound to offend the teacher in one way or another.

Conversation Starters to Use

- Timing between activities is an important aspect of instructional delivery. Your delivery is solid, but we need to get the timing from the desks to the carpet improved. You might use a sing-song approach where when the song is done, they're all seated. I've heard this one used and it's easy for kids to memorize: "Criss cross applesauce, hands in your lap, don't say a peep, and don't take a nap, smile at your teacher ... and give a big clap." This is just one example of a song to use. Let me know when you plan to use this strategy and I'll come back to observe.

- You do a great job with the Smartboard and its features. We need to get your students to the carpet in a quicker and more orderly fashion. The board has a timer that you might set as a visual for how long you're allotting them to move from one area to another. It took you about two minutes today, and it should be more like 30 seconds. See if the timer helps, and I can come back to observe next week.

- Mrs. Smith, during the transition, you had to give students the directions three times. We need to get that down to one time only to improve transitions and prevent the loss of instructional time. One suggestion I have is to praise students who are acting and following directions. This is an effective way of correcting non-compliant students. For example, "Victoria, I love how you're following directions, please turn your card to blue." Since you have a behavior chart this would work. Let me know when you have this down to a science, and I would love to come back and see the improvements.

- We need to get better timing from the desks to the carpet. Try dismissing the students in waves, letting them move at different times rather than all at once. This would eliminate the mass rush and allow you to incorporate your attention-getter when they're all in place, such as "one, two, three eyes on me," or "class, class," "yes, yes."

These four conversation starters are specific in that they note the problem and then support the teacher with a specific suggestion. The suggestions are not complex or complicated to put into practice. In fact, the teacher could use any of these the next day. Notice, too, that Mr. Ames is inviting himself back to make sure that the improvements to timing and transitions are taking place. None of the suggestions are offensive, but they are candid about the fact that Mrs. Smith needs to put these in place and that it's an expectation that she do so. A less effective approach to bringing the problem up for conversation and professional dialogue is in the use of questioning, which leaders often do when they're stuck in the circle of nice. Take a look at the following questions we suggest you don't use.

Questions Not to Ask

- How could you improve the transition to the carpet?
- What strategies do you have in place to guide students during transitions?
- How do you use your behavioral chart to improve behavior?

The first two questions are leading questions that potentially set up a confrontational situation considering the teacher didn't have a strategy for a smooth transition. They're ambiguous, leaving the teacher thinking "Does she think my transitions need work?" They're also not helpful. It's simply not fair to the teacher to ask the question, "How could you improve?" when you're thinking that she needs to improve. And, it assumes that she knows how to improve the transition but she simply failed to do so. Assuming that the teacher has the skill but not the will is a dangerous assumption. It's like assuming a carpenter has the skills to build a solid structure but built one that fell apart just because he didn't feel like putting in the effort. It sets up the conversation and subsequent dialogue to fail when it's likely done to be "nice" instead of being candid, which is the only way to improve performance.

The third question might work in a post-observation face-to-face conversation, but in email or walkthrough feedback it has the potential to offend. Mr. Ames didn't see the behavioral chart being used and the student behavior needs addressing. It's more effective to say something like, "I would have liked to see the behavior chart used when your students didn't follow your directions. Maybe I'll see that during my next visit." In this candid approach, the expectations are clear for Mrs. Smith and it demonstrates evidence that the chart was not used. The evidence is objective and the expectation is well established for future improvements. Let's take a look at what the observer could have said if he used a candid approach.

What the Observer Could Have Said with Candor

Mrs. Smith,

The mini-lesson on the How To writing piece was well developed. The modeling and examples, which were organized and displayed well on the Smartboard, were excellent, effective and well thought out. Your instructional organization prevented unnecessary questions and the students understood the lesson. In addition, it was also great to see the effective use of the Smartboard so that your students understood the How To through visuals.

Regarding classroom management, the transition to the carpet needs improvement and should be seamless. I've seen the following strategies in use and you might employ one or more of them to improve transition times:

1. Praise students who are transitioning correctly rather than correcting those who are not, such as, "Victoria, I love how you're following directions, please turn your card to blue." Since you have a behavior chart this would work.

2. Use a transition sing-along to get the group moving and participating as quickly and orderly as possible, such as "Criss cross applesauce, hands in your lap, don't say a peep, and don't take a nap, smile at your teacher … and give a big clap." Once students have this memorized, it can work to get them seated by the time they're done singing. It's quick, it's fun, and it provides the needed order to prevent the loss of instructional time.

3. One more strategy that I would suggest is to dismiss different students at different times rather than all at once. This would eliminate the mass rush and allow you to incorporate your attention-getter when they're all in place, such as "one, two, three eyes on me," or "class, class," "yes, yes."

I'm looking forward to coming back to see one or more of these strategies in place. Your students are learning so much from you

(Continued)

because you plan so well and use great instructional practices. The next step is to tighten up these transitions to maximize the instructional time. Let me know if you want to talk about these strategies.

Here's a Tip

Tell the whole story.
Note the improved candor and the support for the teacher in making improvements to her transitions. Note also that Mr. Ames simply says more. To think something about someone and to not tell them is not fair, especially from the perspective of the supervisor to the teacher. We're calling for "the truth, the whole truth, and nothing but the truth" as an approach to informal feedback to teachers. The worst thing would be to conduct walkthroughs all year, thinking about missed opportunities in classrooms, fail to tell teachers how they can improve, and then document improvements needed in formal evaluations. Be upfront and early with your suggestions to teachers so that they can improve prior to their formal evaluation, and never gloss over a missed opportunity to provide direct feedback.

Candor Cancellation #3—*The Excuser*

In this scenario, Mr. Ames doesn't make any excuses for the students being out of control, and in the improved feedback, he's direct. His problem is that he doesn't target the issues he encounters. But we find leaders who make excuses galore for teacher performance, especially classroom management. We often hear teachers and administrators say things like "this is a tough group" or "this mix is difficult" or "this is a large class." Don't be a leader who makes excuses for teachers or students. Doing so projects blame, which won't help the situation. Making excuses diminishes high expectation and cancels any candid statements that would follow the identification of an issue or a highlight of a classroom visit.

Conclusion

Each scenario in this chapter provides the observer with a challenge in considering that there are elements to each lesson that are good but that each also has areas to improve. That is often an obstacle for observers since they have a tendency to accept good practices rather than striving for great ones. We have learned from Jim Collins that "good is the enemy of great" (Collins, 2001). If observers want to improve teacher practice and maximize the best practices through the use of informal feedback, they have to consider the following:

1. When leaders know what teachers need to do to improve and they don't come right out and say it, they're accepting status quo in schools, which isn't fair to students.

2. When leaders hold back on the frequency and amount of feedback they give, it creates teacher disengagement through a lack of quality professional dialogue.

Candid feedback, in a culture of compassion and support, represents a push toward continuous improvement, something that our best teachers strive for on their own but genuinely welcome from others. But, feedback is generally only welcomed when it's useful. There has been a great deal said about building trust as a leader, but we contend that trust can only occur through candor. In other words, you don't build trust so you can be candid, you build trust by being candid. That can't happen if the focus is on being nice rather than being helpful.

Scenario one reveals an issue with the teacher's choice of instructional strategy, scenario two deals with the teacher using the instructional strategy in an effective way, and scenario three addresses classroom management. In all three scenarios, the observer encounters quality teaching and learning but also notices the need for improvements. We find major differences in what the observer thinks and what the observer says. The improved feedback bridges the observer's thoughts with the informal feedback to the teacher, which has a far better chance of improving practices in the classroom. The biggest differences are in the specificity of the feedback, the length of the feedback, and the candid approach to what we're willing to say to teachers during classroom visits. This brings us to the three leadership pitfalls that are common when giving feedback to teachers—*The What,*

The Out, and *The Blame*. The first, The What, is a problem with identifying, with accuracy, the true problem and then pointing that out for the teacher. Leaders find this pitfall when they hold back their thoughts or word them in a way that doesn't address the whole concern. The second pitfall, The Out, is when leaders provide an easy way out so that nothing has to change. In the scenario we posed, The Out presents itself when the message is so unclear and ambiguous that no one could be expected to take action as a result of it. The third, The Blame, is when leaders blame something— temperature, day of the week, group of people, etc.—for what's going on in the classroom, taking the control away from the adults, who make the biggest difference in the lives of students, and often making excuses for poor performance. All three cancel out any attempt at providing candid feedback for growth during walkthroughs and instructional rounds.

Earlier in the chapter, we made claims about informing walkthroughs with instructional rounds to maximize these best practices. We've made the leap from weak walkthrough feedback to that of a more candid approach, but we still need to draw big-picture conclusions about school-wide improvements. In these scenarios, the observer can improve each individual teacher's practices, which is the point of conducting classroom walkthroughs in schools. But what if she can also draw conclusions about needed improvements school-wide, which can be addressed in newsletters, at faculty meetings, and during PD days? If the observer is willing to invite teachers to conduct rounds to collect evidence about levels of rigor *or* questioning techniques *or* student engagement, more can be said to the collective staff about what they all can do to improve practice. The rounds, then, inform the observer for the more granular level during each individual visit. District office staff should consider supporting principals and other observers through the use of rounds. By conducting rounds with curriculum office personnel and principal supervisors, we can inform observers in their efforts to provide the very best feedback to teachers possible.

Again, this chapter of the book focuses on teachers receiving written informal feedback. Add to this a systematic way to have face-to-face interactions and you'll really be kicking your candid approach up a notch. We address more about face-to-face meetings, including a collaborative decision-making approach, in the following chapter. We hope you'll take the steps to communicate outside the circle of nice in your school.

Collaborative Decision-Making

Leading Effective Meetings and PLCs

Introduction

In our Preface and Introduction, we set the stage for this book and a candid and compassionate approach to using school and district leadership strategies so that you can step outside the circle of nice while remaining compassionate, but with a more effective approach to leading your school or district. It's imperative that you read both before reading any single chapter of this work. As we discussed, you can read each chapter separately as long as you read the Preface and Introduction in their entirety first. We want to be sure that our terms and purpose are consistent as we describe how each of these three best practices—informal feedback, collaborative decision-making, and teacher leadership—will only work with a candid approach.

This chapter is dedicated to collaborative decision-making, a process touted for its inclusivity and typically regarded as a productive best practice in schools. Collaborative decision-making involves bringing together the people who have direct contact or responsibility over the resulting factors of the decision being made and working together toward a common understanding of the next steps in solving a problem or carrying out an initiative. Leaders should consider forming a team of people who care most about any organizational issue or project as the collaborators for decision-making for that project (Kotter, 2014). In schools, collaborative decision-making comes in the form of specific committee work, school steering committees, or leadership teams. These groups hold meetings regarding various topics that require decisions to be made for progress to ensue. However, establishing the committees and selecting the right people is the easy part. Too often, collaborative decision-making teams find themselves stuck, unable to make progress, mired in debate or arguing a number of points that may or may not even be tied to the main topic. Collaboration and thoughtful dialogue require skillful communicators and solid meeting structures forged in candor. To ensure success, meetings must have the following key elements:

1. Vision
2. Norms
3. Synergy
4. Trust

Each of these elements are only effective if candor is used throughout and understood by participants. The problems that often stifle progress during meetings stem from a lack of candor because people often either gravitate toward the circle of nice to create harmony, shut down because they feel overlooked, or argue because they don't know how to be inclusive; however, candor opens the door for open and productive discourse. We contend that when the process comes together with real candor and open dialogue, the result is a better decision, communicated through compassion for everyone involved.

Collaborative decision-making in schools should also be a key aspect of professional learning communities (PLCs). The traditional environment where teachers worked in isolation or were given limited time to discuss lessons and strategies with other educators is being challenged by the structures of PLCs in schools. This is a positive approach to collaboration, and the research guides the conversation around bringing teachers together to plan and review data for the purpose of a lesson-study-style collaborative approach. The structures are not the issue, though. The issue is that these structures won't work as a best practice unless candor is woven into the fabric of the conversation.

DuFour and Marzano (2011) discussed the fact that school-based total autonomy doesn't work, but in that same vein, top-down decision-making doesn't prove effective either. Schools need direction and a set of expectations whereby they know the "fundamental goals, the strategies for achieving those goals, and the indicators that will be used to monitor progress toward the goals" (DuFour & Marzano, 2011, p. 29). Beyond that, schools need the freedom to implement within the context of their unique environments. This takes collaboration among leaders within the school, including teacher leaders and other influencers. Principals cannot do the work of leading a school on their own (Fullan, 2014). This means bringing together teams, whenever possible, to tackle the toughest issues that schools face, and when teams come together with common purpose, compassion, and candor, decisions are made faster and with far more clarity than when decisions are not focused, made in isolation, or without a candid approach to the problem.

Bringing teams together in schools is defined by selecting and assembling a representative group of other stakeholders, who have influence after the meeting, and brainstorming ideas until a common thread emerges and a decision can be made that everyone will then support. But it doesn't mean that all of the collaborators have a say in the final decision. Shared decision-making is about input and being able to live with the outcome because we know that the key people weighed-in on it with real "say," which means that if the outcome doesn't work or falls short, the key people will be brought back to the table. Leaders who value shared decision-making, like Lencioni's fictional character Kathryn, know that consensus is not as important for buy-in as is providing a platform for input from the key players (Lencioni, 2002).

With that said, bringing the right people together for effective collaborative decision-making is only the first step. Group dynamics can be complex. In fact, "making good group decisions can be hard, and the difficulty sometimes makes us wonder whether it is worth the effort" (Sunstein & Hastie, 2014). This is why it's critical for leaders to establish certain criteria for group decision-making and set the tone before proposing a problem that needs solving. High-performing teams follow the established rules to govern their work so that the team stays focused on the topic or problem, and the result is an informed decision. Great teams remain centered and don't meander away from their common goals (Murphy, 2016; Maxwell, 2013). When collaboration fails, it's usually due to lack of clarity on their purpose, a breakdown in the established group norms, a missing outcome-oriented interactive thinking process, or diminished trust among the team members. Leaders can overcome all four with candid and compassionate direction and feedback at meetings.

Collaborating for Successful Decision-Making

Collaborative decision-making in PLCs and other team meetings will fail to be productive if the right communication methods are not established ahead of time and used with fidelity. This means that the leader of the team needs to be clear on four important aspects of group decision-making: 1) It's necessary to have a clear vision for the teamwork and outcomes of the group; 2) Groups need norms to be able to interact effectively; 3) A process for thinking and vetting ideas is important for groups to review and select their best options; and 4) Trust is necessary for groups of people to do their best work. Let's explore all four aspects and how, even with these four ingredients, groups fail to move forward without establishing a communication structure that supports candid feedback among team members. The first challenge is that principals who desire a teamwork approach need all four elements to be in place, and the second challenge is ensuring that candor is a fundamental aspect of communicating throughout the decision-making process. Shared decision-making is a well-known best practice in schools, but without the appropriate structure to support candor, the process is compromised, preventing great ideas from being discussed.

A Clear Vision for the Work

Groups need purpose and clear direction. Collaborative decision-making is most effective when the decision is grounded in a vision and core values that the group agrees to keep at the forefront of the conversation. Sinek (2011) demonstrates how leaders need to inspire action with a clear purpose. He says that because "behavior is affected by our assumptions or our perceived truths," we end up making decisions based on what we think as individuals versus the reality of the larger context. This is why having a clear vision is vital for teams charged with a decision to make. The group's dynamic—attitude, behavior, and intention—has to reflect a clear set of "truths" about their work and what they need to accomplish based on the predetermined goals.

"The only way to have your team aligned—moving in the same direction at the same speed—is to develop a detailed vision of the future and share it with them" (Herold, 2018). Principals who desire a shared approach to decision-making have to start the process in one of two ways. The first creates an opportunity for the team to gel organically by allowing the team to grapple with their purpose, clarifying the reasons why they are gathered together and the outcomes they are intended to have based on a topic, idea, or responsibility. The second method is for the leader to simply communicate the purpose for the group, the desired outcomes, and then entrust the group to accomplish the task. Interestingly, most groups will respond to either strategy—working to develop a clear vision on an idea or accepting the principal's predetermined direction. The point, though, is that prior to the group tackling a specific task, shared decision makers need a clearly defined vision to fall back on and to measure their ideas against as they proceed with a laser focus.

To illustrate this point, let's consider a few examples of a vision for collaborative decision-making that schools grapple with all the time. As we noted earlier, professional learning communities are challenging the isolated approach to the traditional lesson planning structures that are common in schools, especially secondary schools where teachers often have unique schedules and distinct subject matter. But, as DuFour, DuFour, Eaker, Many, and Mattos note in their 2016 version of *Learning by Doing*, too often the excuses to not form PLCs or in merely "flirting with PLCs," versus the commitment it takes to make them work, are grounded in a misunderstanding of why a group approach is so important. The authors suggest that the problem is not in *the how* of PLCs but rather *the why*, which strengthens the principal's need for a clearly articulated, unwavering vision.

To anchor the work in the vision, when the teams of teachers come together in a PLC, the vision has to be revisited each time. In the first few seconds of the PLC and then again throughout the meeting, the principal or teacher leader needs to communicate the purpose for the work. Vision statements make a difference by serving as meeting "guardrails" to en-sure everyone stays on track. Take for example this vision statement for 7th grade science teachers: *The vision for our science PLC is to address the standards by collaborating on common lessons, common assessments, and common outcomes so that we can review student work and student data to continue our cycle of improvement with teaching and learning.* Using this example to start a PLC and to refocus the PLC anytime the group members get off task allows for a unified purpose for all of the decisions that get made when the team comes together to collaborate. The problem is that PLC vision statements are all too uncommon in schools, and as such, candor around their usage is simply absent. It's statements like this one that are needed at the start of any meeting where shared decision-making is an intended outcome, but a shared vision is only the first step.

Developing Group Norms

How we interact with one another is as important to reaching our goals as why we came together to interact in the first place. Without norms, meetings can quickly go awry. Some group members tend to dominate the conversation while others disengage and can get off task. Norms are crucial elements to team dynamics because they allow our actions to be backed by a set of agreed upon relationship indicators. It's our relationship to the team that matters most and not necessarily what we would otherwise consider acceptable in a social setting. "Those key relationships, and the motivations and emotions that drive them, are at the heart of an architecture used by the most highly effective teams" (Hurley, 2017).

Norms should be synonymous to the regularly expected actions, attitudes, and practices of teammates. In fact, once the team has a list of group norms, it's important to actually "turn them into measurable behaviors" (Nawaz, 2018). This keeps everyone clear on how to engage with the decision-making process in a collaborative way. Unfortunately, many established group norms are mere words on a sheet of paper. Decision-making groups don't rely on the power of group norms as they should, and we have found that school leaders often establish norms but don't use them to guide and direct the conversations. Rather, the leader uses them as a way to passively address misbehaviors he hopes to avoid from individuals who don't act appropriately. Group norms have the power to take precedence over individual and personal preferences for how some people want to interact with others, but it requires a skilled leader to capitalize on the potential of well-developed group norms.

To make the case even stronger, let's consider the PLC situation we encountered above. We bring together our PLC for the purpose of planning lessons, looking at data, and making collective decisions about what to do when students understand the material and what to do when they don't. We have a clear vision that drives our work, and now it's time to dig into the decision-making process. Let's consider that one of our norms is "equal participation" among group members. We would then expect everyone in the PLC to contribute to the work without one person taking control and unilaterally being allowed to influence the lesson development that everyone else teaches. When the individual begins to hijack the meeting and over-assert his control and influence, PLC members, particularly the leader, have the social backing to "call it out," using the norms as the basis for holding each other accountable.

In this example, one group member might say that she doesn't feel that her contributions are being considered, or even the opposite, where she feels that she's contributing too much and needs more assistance in the lesson plan creation. Due to the various personalities within any given group, norms allow group members to express more of what they need from the social interactions and avoid dangerous assumptions regarding other group members' intentions. This differs from typical social situations that don't have set norms. Norms allow for otherwise socially odd behaviors to be normal so that our shared decision-making process is productive.

Using Systems and Design Thinking

One typical problem with bringing people together to make a collaborative decision is that we actually come to conclusions too quickly. Often, our quick conclusions don't address the whole problem, becoming symptomatic bandaids rather than root-cause solutions. Although this books is not intended to be the holy grail of how to think better or teamwork, we do offer two important aspects to collaborative decision-making that need to be in place and understood by team members. First, the team should understand systems thinking, and, second, the team should use a design thinking process. *Systems thinking* establishes the unique cause and effect nature of every decision and how decisions have both intended and unintended consequences. As a result, groups conceptually and contextually understand how all of the moving parts of the organization make up the whole. *Design thinking* is an iterative process so that the team engages with ideas and questions long before making a decision. "Design thinking is the opposite of group thinking, but paradoxically, it takes place in groups" (Brown, 2009). Let's briefly consider why both are important and why they're needed to set the context for candid conversations.

Systems thinking is critical to understanding the problem that the group is trying to solve before getting to the conversation about the possible solutions. Systems thinking is different from conventional problem-solving because it takes more of a holistic approach versus the typical problem–solution linear type of processing. The difference is in considering problems and their causes (conventional) versus relationships between the moving parts of a problem (systems) (Stroh, 2015). Most importantly, systems thinking takes the decision makers from a short-term fix to a long-term solution to problems. It's the first step in establishing a thinking model after the group has a vision for their work and norms for engagement. Leaders who want their team to think hard about an important issue should be keen on systems thinking so that the team can think big, and as Daniel Kahneman puts it, "think slow" (2011).

Design thinking is the second step where a truly iterative process occurs when trying to make a collaborative decision at a meeting or PLC. Design thinking comes in many shapes, sizes, and colors, depending on where you get your information about it. But it generally appears in four stages and forms: gathering, ideation, prototyping, and storytelling. In general, it means asking a ton of questions, pushing beyond obvious solutions with innovative ideas, building models to demonstrate the new direction, and telling relevant stories to compel others to believe. It's about using empathy to gain clarity and understanding and finding new meaning to direct a desired change in people or processes. As authors Lockwood and Papke (2018) put it, "the use and application of design thinking in organizations appears to be as infinite as our collective imaginations can take us."

Consider an example of systems and design thinking, working together, as a team of teacher leaders try to solve a problem collaboratively. Suppose a principal asks a leadership team to solve a common issue, whereby groups of identified students, even after interventions are in place, are not making expected growth. Typical linear thinking without a systems or design approach usually leads teams to consider different interventions and possibly even increasing their time in the subjects where they aren't making gains. But what if more time and different interventions are really more of the same.

Suppose the team takes a systems approach, thinking bigger than just the subject matter and student scores. Design thinking requires its users to ask more questions, first, to gather as much information as possible. What else do we know about these students? What story can we tell about them individually and as a group? What is the data not telling us? Who knows where the answers to a multitude of questions will lead. Maybe it turns out that only a few of the students are connected to school outside of the regular school day. Perhaps only a few of them have mentors. Maybe the lack of academic progress isn't going to be solved through more academics and interventions but rather through stronger ties to school and meaningful relationships with adults. Suppose the team lands on a solution that gets the students involved in extracurricular activities and assigns them a mentor devoted to improving the students' dispositions towards school and learning. Far different than more RtI. But that's only going to happen if we operate in a group with a clear focus, guided by strong norms, grounded in trust with one another. Trust allows for clear, candid communication since the intentions of the group members are never in question and participants feel safe. The bottom line is that "when it's safe, you can say anything" (Patterson, Grenny, McMillan, & Switlzer, 2012).

Five Ways of Trust

For collaborative decision-making to really be effective, trust is a critical factor. Almost no one is willing to collaborate and share in a decision with people who can't connect through an honest relationship. Trust is precarious. It's very easy to lose, even after developing it over time. However, "the many tensions that surface in the principal's work in a school day are more creatively and effectively resolved when adults work together as a healthy community" (Ackerman, Donaldson, & Van Der Bogert, 1996). As a result, principals must develop this environment to lead effectively. One way to achieve this is by demonstrating trust in the community, which will yield trust back from it. Yet, many leaders don't take an active approach to building trust. They fall into a trap, believing that trust is only earned over time through relationship building. But if you really want someone to trust you quickly, simply demonstrate trust first. Rather than waiting for someone to earn your trust, just give it to them. If both sides are skeptical, as is often the case, it requires the leader to take the initiative and avoid uncertainty and suspicion.

Trust is critical in PLCs and meetings where collaborative decision-making is the goal because trust is the lubricant whereby sharing is the hinge. The greater the degree of trust, the quicker and more effectively the sharing can occur. Sharing is the hinge for collaborative decision-making because when everyone at the table communicates his or her perspective, a better decision can be made. Effectiveness hinges on the best decisions. In fact, the more diverse the group and the more sharing they do, the more focused they'll be, the more careful they'll consider facts, and the more innovative the outcome (Rock & Grant, 2016).

But trust is not a one-way system for leaders who care to assemble collaborative teams. We contend that leaders have to be able to build and maintain trust in five important ways, and they get harder exponentially as we explore each in our five-point trust model below:

1. *Build trust between the leader and someone else.* Leaders have to be able to build trust between themselves and each member of their team. Great leaders know how to build trust quickly, and they know the power of trust each and every time they meet someone new, hire someone new, and encounter new stakeholders. The best leaders know that this is actually the easiest way to build trust because it's mostly dependent upon your personal behavior and individual interactions with others.

2. *Build trust between two other people.* Leaders know how to bring two people together and build trust quickly between them. When a leader knows that two people need to connect with a bond for a collaborative approach, she works to build the trust between two people by finding common connections. Just in the way that we build trust with others, we can create associations between two people who we need to trust one another for a collaborative decision to be made.

3. *Build trust between team members.* Harder than building trust between two people is actually creating a warm and trusting environment within a team of people who need to work together to share ideas to solve a common problem. If you've ever joined a team of people who don't know each other very well, you know that collaborative decision-making can be slow. But, if you've ever been on a team where a skilled leader brought the people together for a common goal, you've watched that leader build trust among the team members, acting as the glue to bond them together for the decision-making process to happen more smoothly than it would without that leader.

4. *Restore personal trust with someone else.* Rebuilding trust gets much harder when you've made a mistake that tarnished your reputation and weakened the trust someone has in you. It takes a great leader to restore trust, using Covey's (2006) high trust behaviors, like righting wrongs, apologizing, and asking for forgiveness. Restoring the personal trust that you once had with another person requires humility, but it can be done. It's vital within a candid environment, where a particular approach may be taken the wrong way. But, broken trust is like a broken

bone. With the right care and intervention it can be reset and restored, and most importantly it can be strengthened in the process.

5. *Restore trust between two other people who have suffered a loss of trust.* The hardest trust to build in our five-point trust model is the trust that a leader has to restore between two other people who have good reason not to support or trust one another. It's one thing to break personal trust with someone else and restore it on your own, but it's something altogether different when two members of a team have wronged one another and don't desire to work together. The leader needs to restore trust and have them come back together for a productive collaborative decision. Sometimes, it's simply not going to happen, but master leaders know how to resolve some of the most difficult conflicts, how to bring even the most dissenting people together for an important cause, how to find common ground, and how to use the goals of the organization to restore the bond.

A challenge with collaborative decision-making is that the people in the meetings and PLCs, the spaces where teams should grapple with critical issues in our schools, don't typically view relationships on a committee through a lens of trust or true synergy. They also don't generally push for a vision, use norms explicitly, or develop a clear process for thinking together. So when issues present themselves, and the vision, norms, structured thinking, and trust are absent, open dialogue, creativity, and meaningful solutions are compromised. It's why problems are slow to be addressed despite the numerous committees and countless meetings to attend. Worse yet, is that even when these four components are in place, collaboration fails to produce a solid team decision because people will hesitate to be direct with one another and will shy away from disagreement if candor isn't at the core. Too often, team members are afraid to say what they truly think or confront "the elephant in the room" because it might offend another member of the team. They hold back from discussing the reality of a situation, which traps us in the circle of nice. This prevents the team from getting to the heart of a problem so that the best decision can be made. You'll see examples of this in the next chapter and how to fix collaborative decision-making with a candid and compassionate approach, but let's first consider why candor is the driving force behind coming to the best conclusions with a team of decision-makers around the table.

Collaborative Decision-Making: Candid Communication

Suppose you have all of the necessary structures in place for successful PLCs and other team meetings—there's a clear vision, established norms, a model for thinking, and an abundance of trust; we contend that your PLC process will still fall short of achieving your desired results and won't work to improve teaching and learning due to a singular reason—a lack of candor. The education profession is altruistic in nature and many who enter the profession desire to improve the welfare of others through schooling. As a result, educators are prone to compromise and to considering the general welfare of others. This is actually what makes the profession noble. However, the downside is that teachers are generally content with being "nice" to one another, and can perceive candor as confrontation. The result is usually concession rather than a win–win (Covey, 1989). When people don't say what they're thinking, to hold back from being too direct with their feedback during the conversation, the product is inferior. As a result, average ideas and mediocre performance, or worse yet, bad ideas and poor performance, are the outcomes of our discussions, mostly due to silence. In Patrick Lencioni's book, *The Ideal Team Player* (2016), he describes a fictional character, Jeff, who encounters the results of a company where "nice" overwhelmed the facts and the realities plaguing the company. Unfortunately, some leaders simply weren't frank enough with their employees, and the outcome was detrimental to the culture, including the retention of top team players. The issue for PLCs is that the outcome should be a quality lesson plan, stronger assessments, and better curriculum for kids. When we hold back, fearing that our comments, ideas, and disagreements will be perceived as offensive, the product suffers and student success is adversely affected. It's that simple: optimal performance requires candor (Dalio, 2017). Candor doesn't imply insensitivity or being rude and disrespectful; instead, it's just the opposite. When individuals are candid in a trusting environment they embrace the philosophy that the goal and the students are bigger and more important than any one person. It takes candor to demonstrate compassion and the distinct care that you desire for people to be the best that they can be (Scott, 2017).

A great example of how candor can forge relationships to curate superior performance is in one of the leading financial institutions in the world,

Bridgewater Associates. If you dig into the company culture, you find that the focus is on people and how the world operates, not just making money. The core of the company is about bringing its associates together to make decisions about how to best invest in the global economy. The result is greater wealth and stronger wealth management, but the process is through collaborative decision-making. The CEO, Ray Dalio, is known for the development of Bridgewater's company principles, and Dalio revealed his approach in his 2017 book entitled *Principles: Life and Work*. In it, he describes a culture of "radical truth and radical transparency." In fact, Bridgewater is far more likely to have a penalty for an employee who holds back an opinion during a meeting than they would a pardon for someone who is trying to be "nice" during a meeting. One of their core beliefs, and what makes them so highly successful in their industry, is their ability to generate productive discourse. Relationships are based in truth-telling and an extreme ability for people to be able to disagree productively. In essence, the disagreement produces a new and often better understanding for both parties, all as a result of candidly expressing dissent. That's what should happen in PLCs and meetings where tough decisions need to be made for the betterment of our schools. We argue that for schools to truly harness the power of collaborative decision-making, and solve ongoing age-old problems that are plaguing the system, they need to embrace this type of Bridgewater culture. They need to create an environment that explicitly aims for candid discourse and compassionate acceptance of everyone's input and ideas.

For this level of truth-telling in schools to thrive, two undermining key issues must be understood:

1. The truth regarding school improvement and best practices is not relative, situational, or dependent on population. Unfortunately, many educators hold on to their opinions, based solely on their past experiences regarding with what works in the classroom, what should be done for a student to be successful, and the approach that should be taken with an initiative. However, the research on what to do in the classroom to support teaching and learning and even the administrative decisions that support school success are very clear, available in the research and literature in our field (Marzano, 2003; Marzano, Pickering, & Pollock, 2001; Hattie, 2009). Actually voicing these research-based solutions at the table, uncovering the problems that are

preventing the implementation of new practices, and aligning them to the particular needs of the school is what is really needed. It's realizing that even in businesses with a lot of subjectivity, there are very solid evidence-based practices that should be at the forefront of every solution. Education has experienced an explosion of research-based practices that yield greater results than our trials of the past. Simply put, these methods and solutions are no longer a matter of preference or opinion.

2. People protect that status quo. Even when we're fairly certain on the effects of quality strategies for solving an issue, we still hesitate to initiate change or challenge outdated practices. This goes back to individuals desiring a pleasant environment, being "nice" to one another, whereby not wanting to offend someone eclipses candor and the need to voice change. This is when people gravitate toward the circle of nice, for fear that their opinion will either illuminate someone else's weakness or it will express a dissension in a way that will be viewed negatively by their peers. What happens, though, quite literally, is that our fear of voicing the truth actually thwarts our ability to improve our circumstances and the circumstances of the students. Amazingly, the most altruistic of people, who care immensely for the wellbeing of young people, create scenarios that do just the opposite. Our choices to not offend, and to create spaces of emotional comfort with those with whom we work, halts and slows down the openness that we need to become better.

Figure 4.1 Collaborative Decision-Making

With that said, strong opinions and even cultures of nice can be conquered by candid and compassionate leaders, those who are willing to champion authentic collaborative decision-making for positive change. Progress and momentum forward, coupled with change in schools, is rare, not because we don't have the tools to create successful change, but because "when neither the leader nor the organization has a history of successful change, then the most likely result of any new change initiative will be resistance, anger, undermining, or simply ignoring the effort" (Reeves, 2016). Fortunately, that doesn't have to be the case when leaders are strong enough to understand and execute the tenements of a truly candid approach to tackling resistance. Leaders who realize that the lack of actual collaboration is hurting the organization are the ones who take massive action toward implementing a candid approach. In the next chapter, we demonstrate several scenarios as examples to guide practice in our schools where we take a less than candid approach by a leader and show you how to change that (Figure 4.1).

Improved Meetings with Candor and Compassion

Examples to Guide Practice

Introduction

The scenarios throughout this chapter are designed to give the reader an opportunity to see and understand how the ideas, thoughts, and research in Chapter 3 can be used in everyday situations. The practical application of skills and key information is what equips individuals to work more effectively. The following sections of this chapter include three scenarios that require collaborative decision-making in very different situations, which are all common within education. Each scenario describes a practical situation, how it is commonly handled by those involved, and key ways the situation can be improved. This is done in a step-by-step process that highlights key changes that demonstrate the difference between success and failure when it comes to shared decision-making and the use of candor.

Scenario One

Leadership Team Steering Committee Meeting

Principal: Dr. Rodriguez
 Leadership team:

- Mrs. Aleyes, Assistant Principal
- Mrs. Smith, ELA Department Chair
- Mr. Barnes, Social Studies Department Chair

- Miss Sanders, World Language Department Chair
- Mr. James, Mathematics Department Chair
- Mr. Simpson, Instructional Technology Coach
- Mrs. Sanders, Lead Paraeducator

The Situation

Over the past three years, Marshall T. High School has embarked on an aggressive instructional technology campaign to outfit each classroom with new devices and equipment so that every classroom is able to enhance students' learning experiences and ensure every teacher has the necessary instructional technology skills. Marshall's campaign, titled *Connect*, brilliantly used three levers to convince the community to embrace the initiative and to support it with necessary funding, which was part of a much-needed referendum. Marshall, the pride of the community, is nestled in a suburban town that is facing serious financial issues. Small businesses are struggling, corporations are not moving in, and the automobile factory sits vacant. Despite this reality, the referendum passed. The town is committed to rebuilding and revitalizing the community and embraced the idea that at the heart of the revitalization plan was investing in its students.

The three levers so effectively employed were:

- *Lever one:* The digital revolution has altered our way of working, communicating, and thinking. Students must have the skills to connect within the school and to a world that is driven by technology, which is ever-changing as a result.
- *Lever two:* The greatest impact on students and their performance is from the teachers. Embracing this reality, teachers must have the necessary resources and skills, enabling them to connect with all students and providing them every opportunity to succeed.
- *Lever three:* Thriving communities that attract businesses and residents have great schools. Great schools are at the heart of thriving communities and *connect* everyone within the community, creating economic vitality.

As a result of the community's commitment, the district allocated an enormous amount of time and money to ensure that Marshall had the necessary technology to achieve the intended goals of each lever. The entire school received a digital makeover. Each room was outfitted for a full one-to-one (1:1) initiative, one device for every student. In addition to student devices, each classroom was equipped with an interactive whiteboard, and other technologies, based on the needs of particular classes. From science labs to math classrooms, needs assessments were made and products were purchased. New equipment and technology was found throughout the building. Items like document cameras were purchased for every math classroom as a means to increase interactivity between the teacher, the student, and the content being taught. In addition to actual equipment, the school purchased various licenses for digital tools to enhance teaching. Marshall was fully equipped, but like many schools purchases alone did not transform the school into an educational powerhouse. Dr. Rodriguez was worried that despite all the time and energy invested, Marshall was not making significant gains.

What is Troubling Dr. Rodriguez?

The initial challenge facing Marshall T. High when they embarked on revitalizing their technology wasn't teacher buy-in, community support, or the district's vision. The financial issues facing the community seemed insurmountable. Unforeseen costs always seemed to arise, and the desire to equip the schools with updated resources always took a back seat. And then it happened, the necessary funds were made available, and the school started executing the three-year technology plan that was designed to bring classrooms up to date, even ahead, as well as to incorporate a professional development plan to be certain that teachers were fully trained to maximize the technology and its effectiveness.

Now, in year three of the plan, Dr. Rodriguez faced problems with the exact issue they meant to address, the effective use of the technology by both teachers and students. Despite the ongoing effort to be a technologically advanced school, and connect with students in a way to increase student achievement, Dr. Rodriguez was not seeing the results. The most pressing issue was that the professional development over the past two years was not finding its way into the classroom. Teachers were not using the skills that they were explicitly taught. Of course, there were pockets of effectiveness, with teachers using the equipment to its greatest ability, but the use of the technology was not as consistent and pervasive as Dr. Rodriguez expected from the outset, and student achievement hadn't improved either. They had set out to do something new and innovative to garner better outcomes as a result, and neither was the case—very little was different in the classroom and the outcomes were the same.

Steering Committee Meeting

Each month Dr. Rodriguez holds a Steering Committee Meeting with key personnel in the school. The Steering Committee is comprised of various teacher leaders, and the meetings are designed to be a place to hash out tough situations for the betterment of the school. Dr. Rodriguez prides himself as a distributive leader. He instituted this model, and he has created high functioning leaders throughout the school who are driven by sound guiding leadership principles. He was confident that his team could embrace the changes needed to ensure that the instructional technology was being used, and he was once sure, at the point when they embarked on the professional development, that the teachers would alter their instruction accordingly. However, he was now uncertain where the issues with implementation and the gaps with usage arose. After the usual steering committee introductions, five minutes of praise (a period of celebration that started every meeting), and covering general information, Dr. Rodriguez dove right into the situation.

How He Actually Conducted the Steering Committee Meeting

"Team, we need to have a difficult conversation around our classroom practices. I'm concerned about the gap between what an instructionally driven classrooms should look like and what the majority of our classrooms are actually doing and how teachers are utilizing technology. Simply put, we could be using the technology much better. Just over two years ago our school community entrusted us with the resources to improve student achievement, improve our students' learning experience, and equip our teachers with tools to be more

(Continued)

effective. The challenge is that despite the infusion of technology into the classrooms, we are not seeing the results. Classrooms look and sound virtually the same as they did before the technology. Honestly, I'm at a loss on why we are not seeing progress. We've provided necessary professional learning to support this initiative, I believe you've championed the efforts, and teachers were enthusiastic, but the traditional sit-and-get method prevails.

I am very open to ideas on how to move forward to make sure that we are making the necessary changes to our instruction. I need you, as the steering committee members, to truly make this initiative successful. And, I don't want this to simply get wrapped up and mired in what we can't do. What I'm looking for is what is possible. To date, I've been in everyone's classroom twice, at least, if not three times, and I'm just not seeing the results. At this point, I want to spend the remaining 30 minutes hearing from you and gathering ideas that you have to improve our situation and get us to where we need to be to accomplish our goals.

On each table you will find chart paper and markers. Please begin brainstorming and writing down your thoughts on how we can take our instructional technology practices in the classroom to another level. Consider the professional development that we've done and what some of you have learned at the national technology conference that we attended the last two years as well."

What Dr. Rodriguez Should Have Done Differently

In our scenario above, Dr. Rodriguez begins with a direct statement, "We need to have a tough conversation," to alert his team that the following conversation is going to be challenging and may cause strife, dissonance, or even conflict. His approach is straightforward, appropriate, and necessary. He lays out what the original expectations were with the technology initiative and then explains how classroom instruction and the expectations don't match. He explicitly describes what is not happening and talks about what he is not seeing during his walkthroughs. He is using candor and clearly demonstrates compassion for his team.

This approach is important for clarity, and Dr. Rodriguez even takes responsibility as the instructional leader that change is necessary and not happening. He is not satisfied with simply acquiring technology; he wants results for students, he wants teachers to grow in their expertise, and he desires to be a good steward of the community. Although he starts off the meeting strong and clear, he makes two critical errors: 1) He misses a golden opportunity to increase accountability among his steering committee members; and 2) He fails to be candid past initiating the problem, which prevents the team from collaborating on the right issue.

Dr. Rodriguez actually needs to take his sentiments further—he needs to be candid about everyone at the table taking responsibility for the problem as a team. And, he needs to be clear about what they need to do about it. The collaborative decision is no longer "how we can take our instructional technology practices in the classroom to another level." He has to make and communicate a decision about the specificity of what they should see in each and every classroom to be satisfied with the usage of the new technology. The pivotal change that Dr. Rodriguez needs to make isn't his willingness to address that there is a problem, or his desire to remain collaborative with the team. The change he needs to make, a common problem among leaders in education, is in his ability to confront the people about their roles in the lack of change that is occurring. He must also move past general technology practices and begin to define, as the leader, what he requires of his teachers. He has to acknowledge the reasons why there is a gap between expectations and outcomes, tie that directly to his own leadership and the teacher leaders at the meeting, and then collaborate on precision. Too often leaders stay general and don't communicate with candor when problems present themselves. Leaders need to choose the right tool to fix the problem, no different than using a hatchet when a scalpel was the necessary instrument.

This changes the tone and expected outcomes of the meeting. No longer is this a brainstorming session to determine possible next steps, but rather an outcome-based meeting with clear goals and expectations for each of the participants. This approach requires the leader to have a keen sense of what the issues are, how he needs to use his team and rely on the trust he has built among them to have a discussion on their role in taking responsibility for the initiative's success.

Collaboration is important to Dr. Rodriguez, but in this instance he is asking for input on information he should already have and likely already knows. There is an obvious gap between his message and what is being done in the classroom, and that gap needs to be closed through instructional leadership. This situation requires a pivot from how he traditionally uses his steering committee, from understanding situations and gaining general feedback on them, to asking them to provide clear and direct answers on how the technology should be used to by the teachers. Collaborative decision-making requires leaders to think about their team as experts, which takes meetings like this one from a general brainstorming approach to specific outcome-based collaboration. Leaders have to leave the meeting with an actual path forward, not just ideas and inputs whereby a decision is not really made.

Although Dr. Rodriguez still needs his committee's input, he doesn't need abstract thoughts and assumptions, but rather concrete solutions and examples. Dr. Rodriguez is at a critical moment where desperate action needs to be taken and his mistake is opening up the meeting to gather ideas on how to improve the situation without a clear understanding of why the problem exists. He needs to clarify whether this is a leadership issue, a teacher expertise issue, or a resistance to change issue.

The essential questions that Dr. Rodriguez must answer prior to the steering committee meeting is why instructional practices are not changing and why teachers are not utilizing the technology. One way to do this is by gathering information before his meeting. This will give him greater clarity on the situation, thoughts on how to move forward, and a better understanding of how to use his team. This approach still allows him to be collaborative but the focus is solution oriented, rather than open-ended brainstorming. Having teams working at tables, generating ideas on a problem that has persisted, will not lead to the necessary solutions. In fact, it will more likely only circle the issue without ever really dealing with the root cause. Dr. Rodriguez needs to know the issue and identify it candidly. The department heads and the teachers in their departments are not using the technology and the specifics of implementation have not been defined. The issue is accountability and everyone is at fault. The problem is that nothing will change, even with attempts at collaborative decision-making, without candor.

Considering the initiative is in year three, Dr. Rodriguez needs to not only be clear about the problem, but he needs to have a better understanding of why there is a problem. This will allow for precise, surgical and tactical decisions to be made. The issue Dr. Rodriguez faces is how to switch his leadership style, and his predominant way of using his steering committee, and still maintain the distributive strengths of his team and their collaborative approach to decision-making. There are times when the school leader needs to make critical adjustments to the plan for any given initiative, and this is where a much greater prescriptive structure to collaboration is necessary for making decisions as a team and achieving the goals of the school. Take a look at the change in Dr. Rodriguez's language below and the candor with which he addresses his team. His compassion for his teachers is clear and he drives them toward a much deeper collaborative process.

How He Should Have Conducted the Steering Committee Meeting with Candor

(Italics represent new/additional text from original statement.)

"Team, we need to have a difficult conversation *around the gap between what is occurring in the classroom with the lack of use with instructional technology and how it should be used.* I'm concerned *about our lack of growth* between how instructionally driven classrooms should function and how the majority of our classrooms are actually using the technology. Just over two years ago our school community entrusted us with the resources to improve student achievement, improve our students' learning experience, and equip our teachers with tools to be more effective. The challenge is that despite the infusion of technology into the classrooms we are not seeing the results. Classrooms look and sound virtually the same as they did before the technology. *Over the past two years we've provided six professional development opportunities, and we sent five teachers to national instructional technology conferences to support this initiative, and I believe we've provided ample support. Unfortunately, the predominant instructional strategy in classroom remains direct instruction with sporadic use of our resources to supplement instruction.*

As a result, I've met with three teachers from each department to gain a better understanding of our dilemma. Although I agree these changes take time, which was a common response among those I spoke with, I believe we can proceed faster by instituting the following ideas to support our original technology plan. We are going to use models to have a clear understanding of what a technology classroom

(Continued)

looks and sounds like. We will build internal support through coaching, and I will be explicit with feedback and reflection that is specifically targeting our expectations during my walkthroughs. It is clear to me, from my discussions with teachers and classroom visits, that we need to get far more specific with what technologically driven classroom instruction means for our students and staff.

What I need your help with is creating examples of what effective instructional technology looks like in the classroom. We will use a proven model, SAMR, but I want us to fill in the specifics with technology, all based on what we learned from our PD and the conferences we attended. Once these strategies are complete, I will need your help to ensure that they are implemented with fidelity in the classrooms in your departments. We will all be taking responsibility for this plan and reporting back to one another about how it's going.

On your tables there is chart paper and markers with a basic graphic organizer. We will commit the rest of our meeting to completing the chart and identifying what the various levels of technology integration look like for each of our content areas. You will be the ones communicating this so let's work together so that we're super clear with what we want to see moving forward" (Table 5.1).

Table 5.1 Technology Integration Plan

Course and Instructional Level	Substitution	Augmentation	Modification	Redefinition
ELA				
Math				
Social Studies				
Science				
World Language				
Elective				

The Difference

Questioning *how* to improve the situation has potential, provided it is asked at the right time, but because Dr. Rodriguez asks this prior to fully understanding *why*, his team's overall ability to make the necessary improvements will be limited. The challenge when attempting to collaborate and gather critical information from a team is in discerning what information is the right information. In this instance, Dr. Rodriguez should not ask open-ended questions to his team when they may not know the answer. In fact, they have demonstrated that they don't. Rather, direct questions on specific ideas will lead to better results. The steering committee needs questions to guide the work, to provide direction, and to create productive decision-making.

In this scenario, Dr. Rodriguez needs to first be responsive to the situation, create a plan of action prior to meeting with the steering committee, and then use his steering committee to execute a new plan.

Essentially, there are three steps in solving this issue, and they all involve candor.

Step 1—Clarity

Leaders need to clearly understand why there is a gap between expectations and classroom practices.

By interviewing staff members with an open-mind to understand the challenges, beliefs, and needs, Dr. Rodriguez has a better grasp of the nuances related to what support the staff will require. He is able to bring this information to the meeting so that it goes from a general discussion to one of specifics. He demonstrate compassion for the teachers by not jumping to conclusions, and he uses candor about the issue at hand.

Step 2—Expectations and Responsibility

Leaders need to communicate very clear classroom expectations and build models as support for implementation, and responsibility needs to rest with the team, not just the person at the top.

Dr. Rodriguez needed his team to be the experts so that they would have both buy-in and responsibility for the outcomes. Often, when people aren't "complying" with a new initiative, it's not simply resistance but rather the lack of a candidly communicated expectation with more than one person taking responsibility for the work. When Dr. Rodriguez shifted his collaborative decision-making to having the team develop clearer goals, he was being more candid about the problem and he was demonstrating who needed to take more ownership of it.

Step 3 — Initiative and Execution

Leaders need to take initiative and use the team for execution.

The role of the steering committee should not be to brainstorm why a problem persists in this case. The goal is to move the instruction forward using the technology, something that Dr. Rodriguez has already identified as a problem. The team needed a plan so that their input about the plan was actually valuable. Once Dr. Rodriguez was candid about the teacher leaders' role and accountability, and he presented a supportive model moving forward, the team could make progress with executing the initiative. Because Dr. Rodriguez initiated the conversation with an outline of a plan and not a general question, he created space for the team to take charge. Too often, leaders confuse collaborative decision-making with abdicating the decision altogether to the team. Instead, leaders need to use the team to gather critical information to make a decision or bring a decision to the team to decide on how to implement. Technology usage was not optional in this case so that part didn't need collaboration; it was the "how" that teacher leaders needed to define for themselves and the other staff they support

Dr. Rodriguez's attempt to include his steering committee is noteworthy and a commendable leadership attribute. And, the fact that he confronted the issue without sugarcoating it is critical. Unfortunately, his desire for collaboration and his candor with the problem falls short of effective because he needed more clarity, better communication, and stronger initiative as the leader. As the authors of *Spark* write, those who inspire and lead have a very narrow say–do gap (Morgan, Lynch, & Lynch, 2017). Essentially, the greatest leaders do what they say they're going to do. In this situation, with a fledgling and very costly initiative that still had promise, Dr. Rodriguez needed to step up and clearly outline what needed to happen and then use his team to support the next steps with execution. This difference in approach will inspire and motivate his team and the other teachers they serve. Too often leaders create perceptions about situations that can be false and lead to poor decision-making, such as "teachers don't want to change," or "this is the result of initiative fatigue," or "people are stuck in their ways," or our favorite, "you always regress to the mean." Dr. Rodriguez's approach starts off strong and then he makes a critical error. With the simple adjustments that we demonstrated above, he can identify the true nature of the issue, create a clear plan, mobilize his team's strengths, and reinvigorate the initiative through candor and real collaborative decision-making.

Here's a Tip

Be clear on the purpose of the meeting.
Collaborative decision-making is challenging, but it is also very rewarding. Great teams are at the heart of successful schools. One critical step in succeeding collaboratively is in the leader's ability in being explicit with his team on the specific topic for collaboration, the expected outcomes from collaboration, and, most importantly, what has already been decided that doesn't need collaboration. Unfortunately, these three areas are often overlooked and can be a source of frustration. Very few situations can shake the ground that a leader stands on like those where people felt their involvement was simply to rubber stamp a decision that was already made. Comments such as, "they already knew what they were going to do," or "they didn't need me, they just wanted to make it seem like we had input," are responses to either poor communication or deceit. We find the former to be more the case, whereas leaders are not forthright about various situations and transparent about what they have already decided and what they need from the team as far as input. Too often, collaborative decision-making is touted as a problem-solving technique when it needs to move past identification to solution-oriented collaboration. Leaders must, then, be more direct, moving beyond the what to the how. Leaders have to say to themselves and others, "I've identified the what but I need the team to help with the how." This candid approach is more effective and gains the respect of subordinates due to the clarity and direction it provides. That's precisely how you can be candid and compassionate at the same time.

Candor Cancellation #4 — *The Generalist*

Don't be a generalist as the leader or you'll cancel any attempt at being candid. Candor requires specificity. Dr. Rodriguez was far too general in his approach to the problem, and although he was candid about the issue, he was never going to get candid about the solution if he stayed general in his approach.

Scenario Two

Third Grade Professional Learning Community (PLC)

PLC members:

- Ms. Jenkins, Team Leader
- Mrs. Tremblay
- Mrs. Ramirez
- Mr. Allen
- Mrs. Simmons

The Situation

This year the third grade team was charged with improving their students' performance on the state assessment, particularly on the English language arts portion. Student performance has declined and the school administration wanted to implement new strategies that could enhance instruction and improve scores. Ms. Jenkins was approached by the principal and was asked to ensure that all third grade teachers' instructional practices become more aligned with their grade level standards. After a year-long cycle of walk-throughs, the principal identified significant differences in each of the teacher's instructional strategies while teaching writing. One teacher, for example, would teach writing using writer's workshop approach while another would be teaching grammar rules in isolation while yet another had no block of time clearly identified for writing and attempted to teach it in the context of other material. The principal was clear that the team needed cohesion and more standardization but wanted to leave that up to the team leader to decide collaboratively what that looked like with her team. Each teacher within the grade level was considered instructionally strong and the principal believed that Ms. Jenkins could guide the work effectively in a PLC where she had some previous experience making decisions collaboratively with these teachers.

Ms. Jenkins, the third grade team leader, presented the situation to her team and let them know what she was charged with accomplishing this year. She asked the teachers how they could become more unified as a team regarding their instruction with a specific emphasis on writing. The team wasn't overly enthusiastic about the request and didn't necessarily agree with the principal's position. Each teacher thought that they were strong in their own way, covered the necessary standards, and did so with different styles. After a few minutes, Ms. Jenkins was able to redirect the group and focus them on coming up with a solution. Mrs. Ramirez suggested that they officially adopt writers workshop as their key strategy. She believed in the process, and because her students' writing dramatically improved over the course of the year on the state test along with the interim benchmark assessments over the last two years, she was convinced of its effectiveness. Since she was fluent with this method of instruction, she offered to develop the plans for the school year and share them with the team. Unbeknown to Mrs. Ramirez and the other members, Mr. Allen was not really in favor of writer's workshop and valued a more traditional approach. Having taught for 19 years, Mr. Allen was convinced that a more prescriptive approach was superior, which he felt yielded greater student achievement results, required less scaffolding and differentiation, and, ultimately, was less time intensive for the students and the teachers. Unfortunately, Mr. Allen did not voice his concern or disagreement in the PLC, and in hearing no outright objections or disagreements, Ms. Jenkins gave Mrs. Ramirez the green light to proceed with the work of creating the plans for everyone.

To fully implement writer's workshop, Mrs. Ramirez developed a year-long curriculum for the team that required a 40-minute writing block each day. Utilizing her own resources and expertise, she spent hours developing weekly lesson plans to guide the 40-minute writing block. The lesson plans included the following:

- The unit objective and a brief description of how the lesson would meet the objective along with the state standard(s) for each lesson

- Daily lesson objectives broken down into "I can" statements for students to guide the writers workshop
- Grammar skills, covered throughout the week
- Mini-lessons that are to be incorporated within the daily lesson plan outside of the workshop time
- Materials needed for each lesson (Table 5.2).

Sample Lesson Plan Structure Created by Mrs. Ramirez

Table 5.2 Lesson Plan Structure

Week of 9/15 Writer's Workshop Lesson Plan					
Day of the Week	Unit Objective	Student Friendly Lesson Objective or "I Can" Statement	Grammar Skill	Mini-Lesson	Materials
Monday					

Needless to say, Mrs. Ramirez invested an enormous amount of time and was incredibly happy not only to help her colleagues but to create something she truly believed in for the students. Once the materials were created, they were distributed to the team by Ms. Jenkins with clear guidelines on how to embed writer's workshops into the daily lessons. Ms. Jenkins also told the team that they would discuss the progress in regard to implementation, to include student work samples being completed, and student growth within their weekly PLC meeting. Her goal was for student outcomes to be the primary topic of collaboration during the PLCs that they scheduled for the year.

What is Troubling Ms. Jenkins?

The third grade team has met every Monday, staying true to their PLC time even when day-to-day issues took hold. They were guided by clear norms at their meetings with a set agenda, and as much as Ms. Jenkins thought possible, they trusted one another as a group. They had trust among their team members and trust with the administration. As originally decided at the beginning of the year, the team discussed their progress with writer's workshop each week. Now, two and half months into the school year and eight weeks of writer's workshop, their stress is starting to build, dissension among the team members is growing, and the demand to conform in their teaching practices is surfacing with complaints. Standardized practices are being called "rigid," as one team member put it, and it's wearing on the team's productivity and patience with each other. Ms. Jenkins knows that not all of the team member are following the plans with fidelity and that her team's morale is diminishing. Worse yet, the principal recently sat down with Ms. Jenkins to discuss their progress with the initiative and to hear how she felt the team was doing. The principal acknowledged that during two or three of her recent walkthroughs, specifically timed during the writing block, the teachers were doing other activities. Ms. Jenkins, believing in her team and thinking that the initiative was sound, reassured the principal that they were on track and that they were experiencing the normal growing pains associated with a new initiative.

How She Actually Conducted the PLC Meeting

Ms. Jenkins:

"Good morning everyone, first thing on our agenda this morning is to discuss how last week's writer's workshop went. Remember, we want to consider this question within three areas:

1. The lesson plan itself
2. How students are doing and growing as writers
3. If you are seeing identifiable growth

Who would like to go first?"

"I will" said Mr. Allen. "I'm not sure this is working. To be honest, I feel like my students aren't progressing as fast as they should be, and I'm not seeing the growth. No slight to Sandy (Mrs. Ramirez), I know she put a ton of time into this, but I don't necessarily agree with this approach. She and I have different teaching styles, and because my students are writing on very different levels, especially the poorer writers, I feel like they are falling behind."

(Continued)

At this point Mrs. Simmons also spoke up. "I have to agree with Bob (Mr. Allen). My students are not ready to have this level of independence. I like the mini-lessons because they are more structured and I think my students need more prescriptive teaching. When we move to the actual writing portion, they get stuck. I would like to increase the amount of time on the mini-lesson and teaching the specific skills associated with writing."

At this point, Sandy, definitely feeling frustrated and a little betrayed, interjected that writer's workshop is a process and that not all students will be on the same writing level. She made her claim that this is about individual student growth. She added, "Bob, there's no doubt that the struggling writers find this more challenging, but it also allows you more time to work with them as writers." Ms. Jenkins, trying to regain some control of the PLC, chimed in, "Bob, there is no doubt that we are all still learning how to do this with fidelity and are uncertain about the outcomes. Which aspect of the writing block do you find most beneficial?"

Bob, seizing the opportunity, responded "Jan, I'm familiar with writer's workshop. This is not about my inability to use the strategy, it's a matter of the strategy's effectiveness. I agree with Elaine (Mrs. Simmons) that the mini-lessons, the more concrete aspect of the workshop, is what I want to spend more time on with the kids. We all know that by time the students get to third grade they have very different ability levels, and my students need a more prescriptive approach."

Then Sandy jumped in, "Bob, I don't doubt that you are very familiar with writer's workshop, but I do wonder about the extent to which you are truly implementing this in your classroom. Each week when we report, you barely comment. I realize this is a change, but I also remember Jan (Ms. Jenkins) asking us what we thought was the best way to move forward and no one spoke up."

At this point, the tension in the room was evident so Jan spoke up as the leader, "Before we go any further, let's take a minute and see where we are with this. We are running out of time and I don't want to end with bad vibes. Sandy, you have put a tremendous amount of work in, which is truly appreciated, and I believe it has made us all better at teaching writing." "There's no doubt," added Bob. "I just don't know why we have to be so lock step." Then Linda (Mrs. Tremblay) added, "We need to be on the same page to measure growth and see if what we are doing is working. If we all follow the same plan we will be able to measure growth. From my perspective, writer's workshop is going really well in my classroom. I like the structure and how we weave in the grammar skills versus teaching them in isolation." Then, Jan added, "It seems like Sandy and Linda like writer's workshop and are happy with the way things are going, while Bob and Elaine want less structure with some flexibility to incorporate strategies and skills as they see fit. Personally, I don't see a problem with us sticking to the writer's block but not having to stick directly to the lesson plans as Sandy designed them. If you see a need to alter them, feel free to do so." With Jan's final decision, the clock read 8:35, and the PLC ended.

What Ms. Jenkins Should Have Done Differently

Open unbridled collaboration is very challenging. It requires an enormous amount of cooperation with a firm belief that the work and the goal is bigger than any one individual. There is a tendency to overlook the challenging nature of meeting in the PLC format because the premise of the group is to learn and grow from one another. However, as ideas are shared and thoughts gain traction, human nature kicks in, and if something doesn't align with someone's ideas or philosophy, tensions can arise. This reality requires a highly skilled group leader, with a willingness to be direct with all participants to keep cohesive momentum going.

Many groups have norms, but as we saw with our third grade PLC team, they were not embedded into practice to govern behavior. Ms. Jenkins starts the meeting off well and reminds the group of the overall goal. However, Mr. Allen immediately hijacks the meeting by answering her question with why the initiative is not working. With new initiatives and changes to practice, this is not abnormal. Mr. Allen has something to say and is obviously at a point where he feels it needs to be said. But after he speaks, he needs to be directed and asked candidly by Ms. Jenkins regarding the specifics of what he feels is not working. Very often, meeting participants will speak in over-generalizations and make all-encompassing claims. These claims may or may not have substance behind them, and it takes a skilled leader to press on the general statements for the specifics or lack thereof. Skilled group leaders recognize this, and they don't let participants derail the meeting. In fact, they don't see that what is being said is an affront. In this case, it is an opportunity for Ms. Jenkins to dig into the issue to determine the real problem. Instead, the comments made by Mr. Allen and Mrs. Simmons actually develop an argument and a stance that influences Ms. Jenkins, which should have created the precise opportunity for her to truly unveil what is going on. Ms. Jenkins has several chances to be direct with Mr. Allen and Mrs. Simmons, to peel back the layers involved with the issue and tackle the underlying problems that are disruptive and non-evident, but she doesn't. She should have used these unwarranted statements to insert candor into the collaborative discussion so that it was productive, but that's not what happened.

Another critical error made in this case is that Ms. Jenkins permits the value of the initiative to be questioned and defended by the teachers. Mrs. Ramirez is the one who confronts Mr. Allen but this is not productive either. Although she attempts to uncover why it may not be working, it only caused more strife in the conversation. The issue is that this type of confrontation between co-workers can quickly spiral out of control, and it happens quickly. Ms. Jenkins should have had more control so that Mrs. Ramirez never had to feel like she needed to defend herself in the meeting and the decision about what to do next. The lack of candor here resulted in dissonance and disgust.

Lastly, Ms. Jenkins provides an "out" for the people at the meeting as it ended and unintentionally sabotages the entire initiative by trying to be nice and smooth things over. By allowing them the freedom to do something different, she creates more ambiguity about the next steps, which will only result in taking the team back to the lack of standardization they started with. Ms. Jenkins may contend that this is a compromise, a win–win, since they keep the scheduled writer's block with an allowance for some leeway with the lessons. But the reality is that Mr. Allen and Mrs. Simmons will revert to what they've always done without any accountability for making changes to the curriculum. Unfortunately, this is a common scenario that only stifles progress and impedes growth.

How She Should Have Conducted the PLC Meeting with Candor

(Italics represent new/additional text from original statement.)

> *Ms. Jenkins:*
>
> "Good morning everyone, first thing on our agenda this morning is to discuss how last week's writer's workshop went. Remember, we want to consider this question within three areas:
>
> 1. The lesson plan itself
> 2. How students are doing and growing as writers
> 3. If you are seeing identifiable growth
>
> *Mr. Allen, would you please start us off this morning?*
> Mr. Allen: "Yeah, honestly. I'm not sure this is working. I feel like my students aren't progressing as fast as they should be, and I'm not seeing the growth. No slight to Sandy (Mrs. Ramirez), I know she put a ton of time into this, but I don't necessarily agree with this approach. She and I have different teaching styles, and because my students are writing on very different levels, especially the poorer writers, I feel like they are falling behind."
> Ms. Jenkins: *"Thank you, Bob, I appreciate your candor, and I wish you had a better week. Before we begin to dive into Bob's experience, I would like to hear from someone else."*
> Mrs. Simmons: "I have to agree with Bob (Mr. Allen). My students are not ready to have this level of independence. I like the mini-lessons because they are more structured and I think my students need more prescriptive teaching. When we move to the actual writing portion, they get stuck. I would like to increase the amount of time on the mini-lesson and teaching the specific skills associated with writing."
> Ms. Jenkins: *"Thank you Elaine. I am glad both of you are willing to share the challenges you are facing with writer's workshop. We all know that the only way we will grow is to be honest with what we are facing. I also want to note that we are not ready as a team, yet,*

(Continued)

to come to conclusions as to why this may not be working. We have quite a few steps ahead of us before we consider another approach to our ELA performance issue. That being said, I don't disregard what is being shared here or take it lightly as we move forward. I know that we are experiencing difficult issues and learning these new techniques is not easy. I also know that we need to pursue this with vigor and fidelity and lean on one another to grow. Just so I am clear, what I am hearing is that the two of you are experiencing these three things:

1. It does not seem like certain students are progressing at the same rate as they did in your classes in previous years.

2. It does not seem like some students are ready for the independent writing, which is a large portion of our writing block.

3. The mini-lessons seem to be working, and are a bright spot in the writing block for you at this time.

I appreciate your feedback; I hope that I've accurately captured your thoughts and experiences this past week. This is great collaboration and gives us areas of need that we definitely will have as a focus in the future as we continue to meet to discuss the initiative.

Before we hear from the others, just to let you know our next steps, I will touch base with each of you to ensure that I have a firm grasp on what is going in your class, how you are implementing the lesson plans, and the issues that are surfacing. In addition, I would like us all to do some investigating and research over the next few days. I'm certain that we can't be the only ones who have faced these issues. I will collect and share what I find prior to next week so that we can have a productive PLC as we continue to identify and overcome new obstacles."

The Difference

The harsh reality is that if someone wants to completely derail a meeting then he will work enormously hard to do so. Group leaders need to be ready to deal with adversity that may arise during a meeting and take control and focus on the agenda, tabling issues that cannot be resolved in a short amount of time. In the original PLC meeting, Ms. Jenkins made some fatal errors that potentially cost her the initiative, team morale, and from various individuals ever going out on a limb again.

In the second example, Ms. Jenkins has complete control of the meeting. Note that both teachers say the same thing in both examples; however, Ms. Jenkins is in control in the second one. We don't presume that every meeting can be laid out perfectly; however, there are key elements to an effective PLC. In fact, we want to introduce two simple techniques for using candor in a collaborative decision-making setting. The first is a simple technique and a great tactic when preparing to get the first piece of input in the collaborative setting. The group leader calls on the first person to begin responding rather than asking for volunteers. This sets the tone that the group leader is directing the conversation. It also potentially eliminates someone from dominating the meeting, which can save time. The second technique is that Ms. Jenkins acknowledges Bob's comments but doesn't validate them in any way except that they're opinions. Instead, she asks for someone else's comments. She even uses words such as "seems like" in her recap to ensure that she's not accepting the points as real. Again, this is a more tactical approach and simple to do. In our scenario, Mrs. Simmons adds to Mr. Allen's claims, however, that is not what is critical here. The important part is that Ms. Jenkins is simply collecting information and will use that to decide next steps to improve their performance. Despite their attempt to build a "case" against writer's workshop, Ms. Jenkins delicately, but poignantly, acknowledges what she heard, addresses that the ultimate goal is to become masters of this strategy, and describes how she will move forward with the information.

This is actually where norms are critical to the success of a meeting. The team fully understands the purpose, which in this case is to discuss the initiative to improve teacher and student performance, not to validate its existence. Yet, many meetings fail to achieve the desired results due to a lack of adherence to the norms or the group leader's willingness to go back to them to redirect the conversation.

Here's a Tip

Preparation is everything.
Ensure the purpose of the meeting is clear and the leader of the meeting is skilled enough to deal with meeting detractors. This goes

(Continued)

beyond simply setting an airtight agenda and builds in goals with clear outcomes. This is incredibly important when meetings are fo cused on delicate issues or topics that are challenging, like changing a curriculum. Conflict is often evident when new initiatives are in their infancy, and it is very easy for people to question their overall value and worth. When early issues surface, and difficulties arise, people may want to simply quit and either pursue a new avenue or go back to the "old way" of doing things. Knowing this requires the leader to be clear on the purpose and outcomes of the meeting to ensure the meeting stays on track and true to its original plan. This is challenging and all the more necessary in collaborative meetings where many voices are heard and opinions are appreciated but may be off topic. It is critical that the meeting doesn't get mired in what's not working or naysayers are given a platform to discuss its merits unless that is the specific focus of the meeting. Preparation is everything when it comes to handling conflict and staying focused, and one tip is to always start with the norm of a "parking lot" poster board, a place where dissenting ideas and off-topic comments can live for later. It takes leadership to intervene when someone starts down the wrong path, but it's far easier if you already have a place to stash the comments without embarrassing someone in the process. Be prepared with regular norms and ways to handle conflict before the meeting even gets started.

Candor Cancellation #5—*The Smoother Overer*

Don't be a leader who tends to smooth things over whenever conflict arises. Candor requires a proactive approach. Ms. Jenkins needed to step in before Mr. Allen went too far and before anyone else expressed defensiveness, which thwarts actual collaboration. The compassionate approach is to accept the feedback as a valid opinion but to maintain progress with clear direction. Smoothing a situation over almost always creates dissension and ambiguity, which simply cancels future candid conversations.

Scenario Three

Principal Supervisory Session

Meeting attendees:

- Dr. Joe Adams, Assistant Superintendent
- Mr. Ron Williams, Principal

The Situation

Wilkinson Junior High is one of the three middle schools in the Adirondack School District (ASD). Mr. Williams is in his third year as principal after working as the assistant principal for five years. Mr. Williams was the easy favorite for the job, agreed upon by everyone at Wilkinson and at the district office. As the assistant principal, his reputation grew as a visionary leader who was also sensitive to the challenges and obstacles that teachers and paras face throughout their day. Amid increasing pressure from the district office to improve English language arts scores, he introduced a reading program affectionately titled *The Bridge* to enhance underperforming students' reading skills who were coming from the primary school and to equip them with the skills needed to close the gap at the high school level. The gains were impressive so far.

When Mr. Williams was named the principal, the Superintendent had high hopes that Wilkinson could improve student performance in the other content areas and mirror the other two district middle schools' performance, despite Wilkinson having greater diversity and a larger number of low-income students. Mr. Williams, an ambassador of student achievement, truly embraced the school's motto—*Learning is a Right, Achievement is a Decision, Greatness is the Reward*, however, now in the middle of his second year, Wilkinson student achievement scores are flat. He knows that they have to improve, both on the state assessment and the district common assessments, and he has tons of good ideas, but he is uncertain about how to move forward.

When Mr. Williams started as principal, ASD instituted common assessments in the four primary content areas as well as in world language. To support the initiative, the district instituted bi-monthly principal support sessions, which are structured for the use of a collaborative decision-making approach to solving problems. The session focuses on the *Data Treasure Troves* as ASD refers to them—Teacher Feedback, Student Engagement, and Student Performance. Each session is roughly an hour long and follows a fairly prescriptive agenda. The first meeting of the month is on the quality of the feedback that teachers receive and the second meeting, at the end of the month, is focused on student engagement and performance data. Each of the big three are broken down into primary categories to help structure the meeting and to ensure that the correct data is used to review progress toward the pre-established goals (Table 5.3).

As Mr. Williams' principal supervisor, Dr. Adams is committed to the success of his mentee and the success of the school. His role is designed around a pressure and support model that clearly outlines the expectations and goals for the principal and offers support to help not only attain the goals, but also to provide any assistance that is needed. Dr. Adams supports Mr. Williams to help him develop as an instructional leader. Although conversations may vary, the overall goal of the relationship is to ensure that Mr. Williams is successful and that the school, through collaborative decision-making, new initiatives, and sustainable resources, aligns itself to the overall strategic objectives of the district.

The principal supervisor role is new in the district and is designed to build, develop, and sustain the growth of leaders within the system. Like many other districts, the school system realized that it needed to develop a principal pipeline and to support those currently in the role. The district office recognized that at all levels, whether a first-year teacher or a first-year principal, working in isolation results in frustration, increased anxiety, potential burnout, and regrettably turnover. The principal supervisor role was one of a few different changes made to increase support to achieve the

Table 5.3 Three Data Treasure Troves

Teacher Feedback	Student Engagement	Student Performance
Walkthroughs	Extra-Curricular Activities	Grades
Observations	Student Conduct	Unit Assessments
PLC Notes	Attendance	End-of-Course Assessments

overall vision and goals of the district. Dr. Adams is in his third year as an assistant superintendent and was an impressive principal in his own right. As a relatively new principal supervisor, only one of his many responsibilities, he is still adjusting to the coaching aspect of the position.

What is Troubling Dr. Adams?

Wilkinson Junior High was in desperate need of a leadership change when Mr. Williams took over as principal. The former principal single-handedly destroyed the trust between himself and the staff. He was often referred to as a HI LO leader—one who Humiliates and Intimidates and is Loud and Obnoxious—causing disruption, fear, and ultimately a toxic environment. Mr. Williams understood that in his first year as principal he needed to repair relationships and restore trust among the staff if he wanted to have any chance of success. He worked tirelessly to improve morale. He made decisions that put teachers back at the table to empower them, he gave them a voice, and he restored lines of communication. As the principal supervisor, Dr. Adams clearly understood this need and championed his mentee's efforts, realizing the school community needed healing. However, now over half way into the third year of his principalship, student achievement remains stagnant and the emphasis from Mr. Williams still tends to focus on the teachers and relationships and not as much on student achievement or his own instructional leadership.

Dr. Adams believes that Mr. Williams needs to turn the corner, pivot, and blend a positive working environment with high expectations, something Williams was able to achieve on a smaller scale as an assistant principal. Holding the staff accountable for student achievement and committing to the vision of the school to ensure the focus is on the expected levels of achievement is the appropriate next step. Dr. Adams, though, is concerned that Mr. Williams is getting stuck in building morale as his only focus, the support side of the work, and not seeing the opportunities for the pressured, high expectations aspect of the job. He appears to be afraid to have difficult conversations with the staff on performance, knowing how fragile the relationships were when he started and all the work he has done to have a good working relationship with the staff. Dr. Adams recognizes that in his role as the supervisor he needs to use the meeting time to collaborate on the decisions to make some changes moving forward, but he doesn't want Mr. Williams to go on the defense so he's conflicted about it.

How He Actually Conducted the Principal Supervisor Leadership Session

Dr. Adams:

"Today I want to review the ELA common unit assessment data from the seventh and eight grades. Ron, I have to be frank. Overall, students are not scoring well. On the most recent test, the average was a 63 percent in seventh grade and a 66 percent in eighth grade. Both averages are considerably low and over 15 percent lower than our two sister schools. We have to focus on improving the scores.

Mr. Williams:

"Joe, I realize we are not where we want to be, but we are making headway. One of our greatest challenges is that the teachers are struggling with keeping pace with the curriculum, and they feel there is not enough time to teach the standards as deeply as they should. In fact, during our last steering committee meeting, we discussed the need to differentiate lessons because our students' scores are so low, causing the teachers to slow down to reteach material, which prevents them from keeping pace with the curriculum. Our options are to either move on despite the students not understanding the material or do what's right, which we feel is to slow down and reteach but possibly do poorly on the district assessment. It's a tradeoff. The issue isn't that the students aren't learning, but rather the fact that there simply isn't enough time to cover all the material before it's time to test them. Switching over to the common assessments, as you know, was no easy task, and our teachers were very reluctant for this very reason. Now with these results, it's evidence that this may not be the best approach for our school. You know we have much different circumstances here at Wilkinson than the other schools."

Dr. Adams:

"Ron, I hear what you are saying but I'm concerned with the scores and now how you are handling the issue. If keeping pace is the problem, then we need to address what is happening here at Wilkinson and what the teachers are doing. Let me be honest, you're coddling the teachers. From what you just described, you even allowed a negative sentiment to fester on your steering team that the common assessments aren't the right fit and that the district office doesn't understand your situation. Not only does this create a division between your school and the district office, it doesn't solve the problem. You are skilled enough to lead this initiative. Standards are one of the only ways we can ensure equity and that every student has the same exposure to a high-quality education. What I am hearing is that we need to lower our standards, not have the same expectations, and permit teachers to not follow the prescribed curriculum. Just so we are clear, that is unacceptable. We meet in two weeks, and during our next meeting, I need to hear some solutions from you."

What Dr. Adams Should Have Done Differently

Dr. Adams and Mr. Williams are in difficult situations. Dr. Adams knows that if the district unit assessment scores are low, then the end-of-course assessments are also going to be low, and since they are all aligned to the standards and can serve as predictors for the state assessment then the scores, once again, are going to be some of the lowest scores in the county. As the pressure is mounting to improve performance, Dr. Adams has a natural tendency to "push" harder and to be certain that the expectations are clear.

On the other hand, Mr. Williams also realizes what the data is saying, that the scores are too low, and that they are not seeing enough growth. Yet, he is faced with the daunting task of raising student achievement scores among students who enter middle school below grade level with a staff that for years has felt unappreciated and alienated. He knows he needs to lead and push boundaries, but as his former mentor used to say, "you can only make change as much as the community can bear or the community will rebel and begin to collapse upon itself."

The above scenario is common within the world of standards, high-stakes testing, low-performing schools, and schools that were led ineffectively. Many schools are confronted with the harsh reality that students arrive on their doorstep below grade level. Whether it is kindergarten or ninth grade, there are always students performing at different levels of readiness. In this situation, the issue is that the teachers aren't following the pacing guides to cover the necessary standards because they feel that the slower pace is better for their students in terms of learning the material. This is an ongoing and difficult situation in schools. Unfortunately, Dr. Adams' approach as a principal supervisor only adds another layer of difficulty. He exacerbates the tension and fails to guide and coach Mr. Williams. His response clearly sets what needs to happen, but, at the same rate, does not address the reality that Mr. Williams is facing. In fact, there are three primary coaching moments in this situation that ended up being missed opportunities for candor and compassion:

1. Dr. Adams needed to first reassure Mr. Williams that the relationship between the school and the district office is one of support and care.

2. Dr. Adams needed to further dig into the data to discover the possibilities that existed to achieve the goals rather than the things that are preventing new and different outcomes for the students, all the while recognizing that there is an issue at hand.

3. Dr. Adams needed to create a real sense of collaboration with Mr. Williams around a plan of action that acknowledges the teachers' concerns but that also equips them to achieve the desired results.

His issue is that he is direct but not supportive, candid about the problem but not candid about a solution. He doesn't communicate the compassion that comes with tackling an issue collaboratively, and he's not even realistic. His position should be to coach. Saying what needs to be said doesn't simply mean repeating the expectations. It requires uncovering the best steps to move forward and coaching with support for a new direction to reach the goals. Candid and compassionate feedback is not just about being blunt, it's about demonstrating care by facing the facts and collaborating on a path forward. We're not saying that Dr. Adams doesn't have the responsibility to point out the leadership missteps of his direct report, but he needs to do so in a way that creates resolution.

How He Should Have Conducted the Leadership Session with Candor

(Italics represent new/additional text from original statement.)

Dr. Adams:

"Today, I want to review the ELA common unit assessment data from the seventh and eighth grades. Ron, I have to be frank, overall, students are not scoring well. On the most recent test, the average was a 63 percent in seventh grade and a 66 percent in eighth grade. Both averages are considerably low and over 15 percent lower than our two sister schools. *Our time today is to focus solely on how we can improve those scores with a plan to move forward together.*

For me to fully understand the situation from your perspective, I want to approach this using a simple four-part review and analysis model that will enable me to understand what's been done to date to support the initiative, your thoughts on whether or not the supports are working, if so are they working for everyone or just some

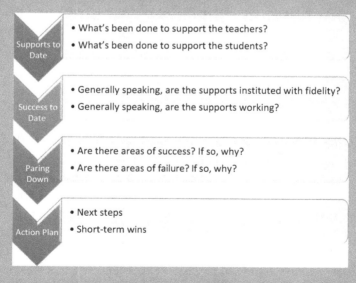

Figure 5.1 Four-Part Review and Analysis Guide

(Continued)

teachers, and, finally, a next steps action plan to helps us move forward. Let's begin with what's been done to date (Figure 5.1).

Mr. Williams:

"Joe, I realize we are not where we want to be, but we are making headway. One of our greatest challenges is that the teachers are struggling with keeping pace with the curriculum, and they feel there is not enough time to teach the standards as deeply as they should. In fact, during our last steering committee meeting, we discussed the need to differentiate lessons because our students' scores are so low, causing the teachers to slow down to reteach material, which prevents them from keeping pace with the curriculum. Our options are to either move on despite the students not understanding the material or do what's right, which we feel is to slow down and reteach but possibly do poorly on the district assessment. It's a tradeoff. The issue isn't that the students aren't learning, but rather the fact that there simply isn't enough time to cover all the material before it's time to test them. Switching over to the common assessments, as you know, was no easy task, and our teachers were very reluctant for this very reason. Now with these results, it's evidence that this may not be the best approach for our school. You know we have much different circumstances here at Wilkinson than the other schools."

Dr. Adams:

"Ron, I hear what you are saying and I'm concerned with the scores. I realize at times that teachers will find themselves falling behind in the curriculum when they choose to reteach material and work toward mastery. In fact, I applaud their willingness to ensure that our students are learning the content and not moving on despite of their scores. Nevertheless, our options should not include abandoning the curriculum guide or spending additional time identifying the problem. You actually had a great opportunity during the steering committee meeting to pivot from the challenges to uncovering some solutions.

There is no doubt that you and your teachers are given a tall order, but I have the utmost faith in your ability to lead them and their ability to achieve the necessary results. You've also developed great relationships with your staff and I believe you can begin truly digging into the issues and searching for solutions. Don't hesitate to steer the meeting into a rich conversation about action steps. Initiatives, in their infancy, are very susceptible to being eliminated too soon because the gap between expectations and early achievement is so wide. Be sure to acknowledge what they are experiencing because it's real, but it is also something that can be addressed. And, that's why I am here as well. Together, you and I can approach this situation as a big challenge, knowing that our ultimate goal is to improve student test scores. If keeping pace is the problem, then we need to address what is happening here at Wilkinson and what the teachers are doing. If you are fearful that the teachers will shut down then we need to look into that issue. But, at no time should the goal, and where we are heading as a district, be in question, which leads me to the steering meeting itself.

To be sure that your steering committee meetings are productive and solution oriented, the last thing you and I want is for the staff to see it as a platform to grieve their concerns. It really should be a team-oriented, solution-driven meeting. You are skilled enough to lead that conversation and this initiative. Standards are one of the only ways we can ensure equity and that every student has the same exposure to a high-quality education. *I don't want to waver from our goals, and I want us to be careful not to fall into a trap where we can't achieve them.*

Let's begin by narrowing our scope of the problem, which is step three in our model, paring down. This is where we can really begin to uncover some key pieces of information. To do so, I want to begin by answering the two leading questions, what are our areas of success and what are our areas of failure? It's vital that we don't make sweeping assumptions, and so we need to deconstruct the data and the scenarios.

(Continued)

1. Of the data that we have, are there any bright spots? Who are the teachers who are finding the most success?

2. Of the support structures in place for this initiative, are they being maximized and do you believe they are effective?

3. Regarding the PLCs, did they spend enough time to establish alignment between the standards, the assessments, and their instruction? Also, have you and your team been able to review the data to begin isolating greater areas of need and areas of success?

4. Lastly, what is the data not telling us? Meaning, what do we need more information about?

Remember, this is about student achievement and working on a path forward together."

The Difference

First, the model, alone, provides more structure and direction for the meeting. This won't necessarily alter what is said, but it does create space within the conversation so that it stays centered on problem-solving and not excuses. Because these conversations can be emotional, the leader of the meeting must provide structure for the meeting to stay on task. This helps everyone involved, including the person leading the meeting. Let's imagine that they covered the first step, what's been done to date, and now move onto success. In our original scenario, Dr. Adams did not handle Mr. Williams' reasoning well. Mr. Williams identified the issues, such as keeping pace with the curriculum guide, the teachers' concerns regarding covering the necessary standards in the allotted time, the students not having the same skill set as those in the sister schools, and the subtle suggestion that the district EOC assessments may be a bad fit. This time, the model provided a way for Dr. Adams to move away from the emotion and stick to the facts about the qualitative and quantitative data they have access to. It also allowed him to acknowledge the perceived issues presented by Mr. Williams without sounding insensitive but with the notion that there needs to be a plan for change. It keeps his candor in place but adds an element of compassion that makes it more than just a blunt response.

The looming question for many tough conversations is how to solve problems knowing that there is not a definitive answer that leads to a clear path forward. Our initial reaction is very often to look for a quick solution or worse yet to place blame or find fault with the initiative or those leading it. As the principal supervisor, Dr. Adams' first step should be to collect more information. Wilkinson Junior High School is facing a very difficult challenge and improving student learning is a major undertaking. The goal in this meeting is to isolate the variables of the problem before jumping to conclusions, something that Dr. Adams failed to do in the first scenario.

Within systems, it's critical to take a step back to see the big picture in order to determine next steps. Dr. Adams' initial approach is to fire back at Mr. Williams and disregard his concerns. He falls prey to the emotional trap and simply barks the expectations with a new deadline, creating opposition and separation rather than collaboration. He may feel as though he's being candid, but he's actually obliterating any space for it to exist. Leaders, coaches, and mentors don't have the right to simply demand results without support. This only leads to frustration, resentment, and possibly failure. The challenges at Wilkinson are not unique, but the approach must be particularly unique in order for the initiative to be successful. Having high expectations is warranted and so is support, collaboration, and a team mentality to achieving the goals together. In the second scenario, Dr. Adams isn't exactly understanding, nor does he accept the excuses. The difference is that he reassures the partnership, looks for possibilities in the data, and creates a sense of collaboration with Mr. Williams.

Within this situation, Dr. Adams gains a unique opportunity to mentor his principal and further develop his skills. He is candid and the expectations are clear, but his method, in the second instance, is much more supportive and far less off-putting. He infuses structure and support while maintaining a very direct and candid approach. This difference is that Dr. Adams is acting as a mentor *and* a boss, not just using the power of his position to dictate. He is clear on the expectations and uses supports to guide the conversation and the collaboration that will ensue. In no way does he shy away from the need to improve test scores or how Mr. Williams handled the steering committee. His approach is actually to deal with both situations, which is even more challenging. Shouting expectations and demanding results actually deflects the accountability from the leader and

creates enemies and opposition. Instead, Dr. Adams needs to take responsibility for the problem with Mr. Williams. If he doesn't, Mr. Williams is
given no other choice but to shield his team from the district office's lack
of support and sensitivity. That all changes with the use of the model, clear
candor, and compassionate feedback.

Here's a Tip

Structure is critical.

Use models to guide the conversation and have a clear structure that
can be referred to throughout the meeting. This is a great way to
keep the meeting on track and to embrace each necessary point of
the meeting. Agendas are good and models enhance agendas. In this
scenario, the model guides the conversations, and because it is a
comprehensive review, it will cover the necessary points, which is
why people tend to jump around. They become off task or move to
other issues that they find most pressing and most urgent. In difficult
situations, this is common and understandable, but can also wreak
havoc on productivity. The use of models that fit appropriately into
the situation allow for a clear plan of action and eventually act as a
historical piece when one needs to go back and refer to important information. It's all about having clear structures for every collaborative
decision that needs to be made.

Candor Cancellation #6 — *The Opposer*

Don't be a leader who barks orders and creates dissension. Candor
requires care and compassion in an effort to solve problems through
thinking and collaboration. Dr. Adams needed to look for bright spots
in the data before making assumptions. He needed to be candid, not
only about the student outcomes, but how Mr. Williams was using
his team. Opposing a viewpoint too quickly does not create the open
dialogue needed for feedback to be accepted, and it simply cancels
our ability to be candid.

Conclusion

Collaborative decision-making is a difficult process that requires a skilled leader to orchestrate a productive meeting. Our scenarios highlight common situations that are riddled by common errors that lead to ineffective meetings, decreased productivity, and negative working environments. Collaboration, however, does not have to be difficult, it simply requires a skillful leader. Meetings focused on making decisions require the leader to facilitate so that everyone is clear on the purpose of the meeting, the explicit norms that we need for social interactions, the thinking model, and the trust we need to work together. With these four elements in place, we can begin to insert candor in a productive way so that our goals are met and our expected outcomes come to fruition.

Our scenarios cover three predominant collaborative decision-making pitfalls that leaders fall into—*The What, The Out,* and *The Blame*. This happens when leaders cancel candid conversations by being The Generalist, The Smoother Overer, or The Opposer.

The first pitfall is The What—a leader's inability to recognize *what* aspect of the problem he actually needs input on to make the appropriate decision. This is a common mistake. Leaders, for a variety of reasons, don't take the time to fully understand a situation or a problem and the time spent on problem-solving is actually focused on the wrong issue or a symptom of the problem and not the root cause. Even if the group arrives at a decision, it fails to fix the problem because it's way too general.

Our second pitfall is notorious and that is The Out—a leader providing an *out* to pacify people. This is typical in high-stakes, high-pressure meetings where the leader is not skillful enough to redirect the meeting participants and simply provides an alternative solution or course of action that destroys the initiative and the original decision. We find that leaders jump to smoothing things over when conflict arises versus using that conflict to drive the collaborative approach or squashing the confrontation altogether. The third pitfall is The Blame—a leader who simply is unable to lead a person or a group to a collaborative decision. The meeting has no space for opinions or voice and is completely one-sided. In our scenario, The Blame approach shuts down the meeting, the principal, and any chance to have a discussion to understand the problem for a collaborative plan moving forward. This creates nothing but opposition, doesn't display compassion, and prevents any possibility of future candid conversations.

All three pitfalls are common and avoidable. The tips at the end of each section are key ways to prepare appropriately for meetings so that you can structure your meetings with vision, norms, thinking models, and trust. Collaboration is a powerful method with the ability to illuminate solutions for complex problems, but it requires multiple perspectives, foresight, and support. The key is going into these meetings with the right tools and the keen ability to navigate the discussions to make the appropriate decision through candid and compassionate dialogue.

Improving Teacher Leadership

6 The Need for Teacher Leadership in Schools

Introduction

In our Preface and Introduction, we set the stage for this book and a candid and compassionate approach to using school and district leadership strategies so that you can step outside the circle of nice. It's imperative that you read both before reading any single chapter of this work. As we discussed, you can read each chapter separately as long as you read the Preface and Introduction in their entirety first.

This chapter is dedicated to improving teacher leadership by taking a strategic approach to leading leaders. Despite an enormous amount of literature on leadership, instructional leadership, teacher leadership, and leading change in schools there is still a great void within the educational system on developing leaders at the school and teacher level. With the wide range of hats that principals wear, it's critical to recognize that the principal cannot improve the school as a lone ranger of decision-making, and assembling a team of teacher leaders is the first step to realizing that schools need layers of support (Fullan, 2014). Simply put, schools need deliberately formed teams of teachers to lead initiatives, to tackle tough issues, and to sustain success. One or two people at the helm will never be enough to drive, manage, and lead the level of schooling necessary to meet the demands of every student with excellence. The bottom line is that schools need teacher leaders, and two problems are preventing teachers from leading better: 1) a lack of leadership coaching; and 2) a lack of effective communication training. Even when teachers are given an opportunity to lead within a school, they rarely get the leadership development training necessary to lead effectively. Even when there is leadership coaching in place, it is often too general and lacks the combination of candor and compassion needed for the teacher to truly maximize their role among their peers.

With that said, not all schools operate with the belief that teacher leaders should be at the table for every initiative, decision, budget item, and change that needs to be made. We contend that decisions impacting the culture of the school, or the effective operations of it, should include teachers, particularly our best teachers who produce the strongest outcomes for students. But, having a leadership team cannot be a facade and, unfortunately, this happens even when teachers are named and positioned as "leaders." The teachers who are designated as leaders must be empowered to lead. They have to lead initiatives, champion decisions, influence the budget, and create change in a way that supports progress and the overall vision of the school. Creating and sustaining forward momentum, especially in larger schools, requires real buy-in and a strong partnership between the principal and the teacher leaders. This extends far beyond simply naming positions and having teachers operate as conduits of information for the administration. This beckons a collaborative relationship that is built on the premise that everyone contributes to the success of the school. Leadership teams are critical to the influence needed on the front lines to make real improvements that genuinely impact the functioning of a school. Behind every great school culture is a positive force, a great principal who empowers teachers to take charge, make decisions, and push forward. This extends beyond just the composition of the improvement team because it also demonstrates and shows that one person doesn't determine the fate of the school. This builds confidence among the staff that they are represented during and contributing to the decision-making process.

"School improvement teams are a regular feature in schools these days. They give staff a sense of ownership over what goes on in the building and present at least the appearance that the school leader alone is not calling the shots from behind closed doors" (Whitaker & Gruenert, 2015). When school leaders aren't calling the shots in isolation, they're deliberately distributing the leadership to their team. By using a distributive leadership model, they establish the foundation for a positive school culture. Spillane (2006) synthesizes the research on distributed leadership practices and concluded that distributing leadership in not simply a "leader-plus aspect," which he considers insufficient since it may overlook the critical nature of relationships and situations. Spillane argues that it is the collective interactions that the leaders experience within the school that matter for a distributive model to work best. This means that not only are teachers leading the work with the support of their principal but that the leadership model is a concerted effort through a shared vision. Distributive leadership does not mean that the responsibilities are distributed to other team members, simply divvying up tasks, but that every team member accepts responsibility in a unified approach.

In addition to understanding the elements of an effective distributive leadership model, it is vital to recognize that leading leaders and developing teacher leaders must be intentional work. Books like *The Teacher Leader* (Tomal, Schilling, & Wilhite, 2014) are written for teachers who want to lead better, but it requires a principal who wants to develop other leaders to truly support an environment where teacher leaders can advocate for and drive school improvement. This is precisely the reason why leading leaders through candid and compassionate conversations needs to be at the forefront of our discussion about teacher leadership in schools. Establishing a leadership culture where candor is present with a true desire to improve leadership practices means leading and developing teacher leaders in a progressive way that views teachers as high-stakes collaborative decision-makers for the betterment of the students.

Leading Leaders

A major assumption in promoting teacher leadership is that great teachers will automatically be great leaders. It's a mistake to believe that the skills effectively used to lead within the classroom will naturally transfer to other situations. There's no doubt that teaching and leading have major similarities, especially in the management aspects of leading groups, but just because a teacher does a fantastic job leading instruction in her classroom does not mean that she has the skills to lead a group of adults in a positive direction. Leadership is a skill that has to be developed through learning and practice in a variety of different contexts. It's an ongoing process that requires constant attention. For teachers who desire to lead better, this means taking on new and challenging opportunities, engaging in leadership conversations, finding a mentor, and even enrolling in a masters or doctorate program in educational or organizational leadership. For principals who propose to develop a team of teacher leaders in a school it means dedicating the time and resources necessary to build leaders and develop their leadership capacity. This creates influence, which is the determining factor in whether or not a leader can move a plan forward.

A key to supporting the development of the leadership team is identifying specific skills and characteristics that need to be developed and creating a training curriculum to address them. In fact, leadership development should be woven into the culture of the school and every team should allocate no less than a third of the meeting time to leadership alone. Otherwise, the rest of the meeting time likely won't matter. We contend that, similar to the Hall of Fame basketball coach John Wooden, who emphasized the fundamentals at every basketball practice, great leaders must dedicate time to developing the leadership skills of his team at every meeting or all the initiatives, meetings, and goals will fall short of their target. Schools aren't short on ideas, knowledgeable people, or even the knowledge of what and how to do in any given scenario; the difficulty lies in the proper execution, support, and sustainability. In other words, if an agenda has a new initiative on it and the people at the table are supposed to move the initiative on the front lines, garnering support and implementation from other teachers without the leadership skills to do so, the initiative will not succeed. It will be swallowed up by the existing practices and molded into a warped version of its original self, which the community will likely accept and tolerate within its current culture of nice. A leader can spend an entire meeting talking about the initiative itself, planning next steps, and get nowhere after the meeting. Or the leader can spend half of the time on the leadership skills necessary to lead the initiative with the other half spent on the initiative itself and expect better results because the teacher leaders possess the skills necessary to influence and work cooperatively with their peers.

Leading a group of leaders is a dynamic and complex process that extends beyond the common skills associated with leading a group of people. Leading people takes personal leadership skills like humility, drive, passion, and emotional intelligence, while leading leaders takes all of the aforementioned skills plus the ability to connect with already gifted and talented individuals who require tailored and explicit leadership development. The best leaders are intentional in their leadership development practices and specifically design and use materials meant to help others learn to lead better. Principals who truly want a distributed leadership model in their schools have to design the leadership learning experiences they want their team to have, decide on how often these experiences can be instituted, and enumerate which skills need to be the focus. The following is a four-point model for leadership development that principals can use on their leadership team and with others who are building leaders who need the competencies to influence situations and scenarios that even the best principals can't handle on their own. Therefore it is a leadership competency for the principal herself to be able to create capacity among leaders in the school and then distribute the leadership for a collective effort. Albeit a useful model with technical guidance, it still requires the leader to operate outside the circle of nice and be willing to give candid feedback to teacher leaders to support their true growth. We address this in the following section after the model, which is then supported by the scenarios in Chapter 7 so that you can see the difference in being ambiguous versus using the balance of candid yet compassionate feedback to transform the best practice of using teacher leaders in schools.

1. Book Studies

The first of our teacher leadership development strategies, and likely the most prevalent due to its ease of implementation for the amount of growth we can experience, is a leadership book study. Think back to our suggestion about allocating a third to half of the leadership team meeting time to learning to lead, and insert a conversation about a chapter of a book that everyone has read. Many teachers are consumers of literature, some of which is in the field of education, but even when the books they choose are educational, they're not usually in the genre of leadership development. This is why leadership development books can make a real impact. A principal who intends to build leadership capacity also has to be explicit about teaching leadership through the use of books during the meeting and not just assigning folks chapters to read on their own.

The next layer to the book study, in terms of the leader's explicitness with helping teachers learn to lead better, is in the selection of the book. One might start with general leadership abilities using *The 21 Irrefutable Laws of Leadership* (1998) or *Developing the Leader Within You* (1993), both by John Maxwell, or dive into a specific need, like trust or team development with *The Speed of Trust* (2006) by Stephen Covey or *Go Team!* (2007) by Blanchard, Randolph, and Grazier. Notice that these selections are from the business arena, making them more obscure as a choice but that much more powerful in the conversations that can occur about application in public schools. Many educators are not familiar with these books so the content can make a huge impact on their skill development and overall mindset toward change and growth. Because many of the school-based leadership books available are about leading initiatives and not necessarily the habits of leaders, we suggest reaching into the world of leadership literature that exists beyond the realm of publications in education.

Once you've selected a book that fits the needs of your team and their growth as leaders, you can study the book in any number of ways. One simple way is to create space on the leadership team agenda to discuss chapters and their concepts, thinking about personal habits and areas of growth in a reflective-journal-type manner. Another way is to assign chapters to team members to present and lead the discussion on that chapter. The point is that the team consumes the literature at the same pace, discussing it at each meeting, and using it for professional development in the area of leading other teachers. What you'll find in Chapter 7 is that book studies are a great place for leadership conversations but they don't take your team to a new level without real candor about what we need to do differently to lead more effectively. One way to achieve this is by tying the specifics of the book to real scenarios that the team or individuals have encountered. This allows the person and the team to view the situation from a different lens, creating space between the incident and the person, which allows for true candor. The situation is the focus, not the individual. This promotes safety, maximizes trust, and helps to avoid getting trapped in the circle of nice, where you can't help the people on your team grow through direct and explicit feedback.

2. Scenarios and Case Studies

The second way to develop teacher leaders in schools takes another simple but very effective approach yet it's not a common practice. We recognize teacher leadership as common practice in schools, but actually investing in leadership development is all too uncommon. Using scenarios and case studies allows teams of people to discuss the options and strategies that leaders could or should use in the scenarios. Leaders can take current and past scenarios from school or district business or even make up mock cases for study. The important aspect of using this as development is for the team to discuss the scenario, why it occurred, and how it might be handled if they encounter something similar. Again, this can be tied to the skills learned from the readings from the book studies, which can complement case studies by providing the leadership qualities associated with tackling issues—like listening better, being humble, being decisive, etc.

We contend that leadership development, especially when done with teams, can and should be fun. Growing as a leader should not be painful. In fact, it can also be *funny*. There are tons of free online videos that can be used regarding what *not* to do as a leader. Snippets from the TV show *The Office*, or clips from the movie *Office Space*, provide fun and funny ways to discuss what it means to be a better leader, a good boss, or how to provide peer leadership. This is also the place for role play. Using scenarios, leaders can role play and actually act out situations as practice for the real thing. It may seem slightly awkward but there's real power in deliberately practicing, using specific language, and reflecting on what it sounds and feels like. A great deal of learning to lead better is hidden because we're often learning to lead as we're leading. Acting and role play with the use of scenarios brings an element of "realness" that books and professional development experiences might not include.

3. Professional Development Experiences

We send teacher leaders to conferences and have them participate in webinars all the time, but we need to also maximize the learning that can come from these powerful experiences by using them for the purpose of leadership development. Teacher leaders are often our most eager learners, ready to soak in new information for immediate application. Most often, they are learning new teaching strategies, new content, new programs, or new ways to manage the classroom, but not necessarily how to be a better teacher leader from the leadership perspective. Even most of the conferences for principals and assistant principals are around initiative implementation, policy changes, and new practices, but not leadership. Principals need to also find professional learning experiences on developing leadership skills for themselves and others. There are several powerful leadership programs that are also offered via simulcast that can accommodate a whole team. However, it is critical to debrief and discuss what was learned. Too often the great information and skills discussed at conferences never leave the conference lobby because we don't synthesize the information and create a plan of action. Great leaders discuss what is being learned and how it can be put into practice by the individual, team, or school.

4. Face-to-Face Coaching

The last leadership development strategy that we introduce is face-to-face coaching. We call these leadership conferences. Just as with a post-observation conference that you would have with a teacher about instructional decisions, praise, and improvements, we contend that you need face-to-face conference time with your teacher leaders, focused on leadership development and learning to lead together. Feet to feet, knee to knee, and eye to eye, these sessions have the power to transform practice as a leader becomes a coach and a boss at the same time, unearthing real potential through guided leadership conferences. The beauty of these sessions is that they can be built using the first three methods we discussed (Figure 6.1).

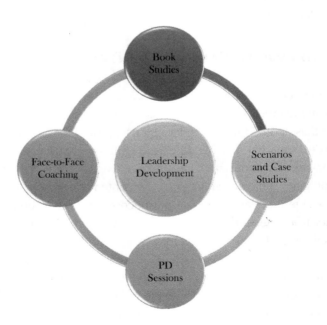

Figure 6.1 Leadership Development Model

Leadership Development: Candid Conversations

Suppose that a school or district leader is invested in developing teacher leaders, using specific tactics like book studies and professional development on leadership skills. Let's even consider that the meeting structures are set up to support leadership conversations at team meetings and face-to-face scheduled feedback sessions that are directly related to learning to lead better for the teachers. We would say that even though the best practices of building teacher leaders are in place, there is still an additional element required or they won't produce the results necessary and desired. The problem is that without a culture of candor and compassion, leading leaders falls prey to the lack of direct feedback that developing leaders need in practice, not just theory, to get better. That's because leadership habits are not quick to change without real intentional actions. In his book *The Leader Habit*, Lanik (2018) described the fact that no one consciously chooses to be a bad leader, but as Lanik found in his research, leadership habits are a result of automatic behaviors, learned from deliberate practice or not. Teacher leaders, or leaders in general, on a quest to learn more about leadership and put what they are learning into practice, have to be placed in situations where they need to exhibit new and improved skill with candid feedback about their progress. This means that leading teacher leaders takes coaching that goes beyond the boardroom book study to demonstrate the skills that the book discussion revealed as necessary for influence, improvements, and positive change. The concept of developing teacher leaders is meant to support momentum in schools for student success. It's only when leaders are equipped with the skills necessary to challenge the status quo, initiate something new, and strive for mastery that progress can be made, which is the very reason why teacher leaders need candid yet compassionate conversations about leading better. And, in the age of instructional leadership and multiple initiative implementation and sustainability, one or two people can't lead a school without an army of support (Fullan, 2014).

Levin and Schrum (2017) noted that every teacher has the capacity to lead if the environment is right and if their skills, knowledge, and dispositions are fostered in a way that allows them to flourish through a distributed leadership model. But their work, like much of the extant literature on teacher leadership, focuses mostly on the competencies of leading well. They end with a chapter on the future of teacher leadership with what school leaders can do to support teacher leadership and even a note about professional development models for preparing teacher leaders. We take this one step further by acknowledging that leadership development has a great deal to do with stepping outside our typical cultures of nice and into those where we lead with candor and compassion. Too often leaders hope their teams learn and grow through well-developed activities and leave success to chance by not pushing the boundaries to deal with the limiting behaviors and the compromising mindsets. The problem is that for these two critical elements of change to be present, it takes a radical leader who is willing to infuse candid conversations into the culture of the school without hesitation or the trepidation that comes with the fear that you might hurt someone's feelings or offend their senses with your words.

School culture is a hot topic. For schools to change from the inside out, it takes a change in the currently established cultural norms, and changing culture can be arduous and time consuming for leaders (Reeves, 2009). Albeit difficult, a leader's primary role is to develop and sustain positive culture, one where the community of learners is behaving in candid yet compassionate ways to challenge members to new heights (Casas, 2017). But, as Casas (2017) explains in his work on school culture, unfortunately the number one factor missing in schools, and even small and large businesses, is "effective leadership." Leaders who are truly willing to face the brutal facts, create agility when things have been stale or stagnate, distribute power to those who seemingly have none, and demonstrate the need to get better as quickly as they can are simply rare.

Limited to only a few businesses who have a true desire to push forward in their industries, recognizing that the investment in their people is an investment in the bottom line, we find IBM to be of interest regarding a culture of candor and compassion. With over 100 years in a quick-to-change industry, IBM pivots like a startup rather than the mammoth company that it is. Shifting culture for any business takes real leadership, and IBM is no stranger to new cultural demands in an ever-changing tech world. But the proof in their model is the commitment that they have to building leaders at every level through candid feedback on performance. With the implementation of their coaching program, more than 90,000 employees use an app that allows them to provide peer-to-peer leadership without taking the responsibility away from managers to do the same (Lebowitz, 2016). The performance management system provides feedback in five key areas: results, client success, innovation, responsibility to others, and technical skills. Users can get feedback from managers, direct reports, and teammates at any time, and feedback givers are supported by new tools to help provide corrective action to others. Because the company recognizes middle-manager and peer feedback as both critical but also difficult, it supports the leadership development of those who are giving feedback on performance, project management, and other functions. The goal is to improve feedback and strengthen a culture of learning to lead better at every level.

This type of shift to a culture of leadership, leadership development, and ongoing feedback is exactly the kind of coaching environment that schools need for sustainable success. But it requires a shift from nice to an environment that thrives on getting better, maximizing potential, and reaching incredible heights through candid conversations and the faith that the leader has everyone's best interests at heart. Teacher leaders need development so that they can be supportive of their peers, and that can only happen in a culture of candid discourse about leading better through the ranks of teachers. In the coming pages, we consider several scenarios where leading leaders through candor and compassion is absent, as is often the case, but we also demonstrate by example how leaders can improve teacher leadership in ways that make a huge difference for the culture of the school.

Candid and Compassionate Conversations to Restructure Leadership Learning

Examples to Guide Practice

7

Scenario One

Teacher Leader Development Session

Session attendees:

- Dr. Collins, Principal
- Mr. Kim, Social Studies Department Chair
- Mrs. Alistair, ELA Department Chair
- Mr. Tennyson, Instructional Technology Coach
- Mrs. Brown, Science Chair
- Mrs. Hall, Elective Chair

The Situation

Over the last three years, Hillsborough West High School experienced significant teacher turnover. Not for any other reason than simple retirement, this once stable, and by most standards high-achieving school, is now watching veteran teachers of 30-plus years shut their classroom doors for the final time. This exodus has brought in a wave of energetic, talented, and inexperienced teachers. In three years, Dr. Collins, the principal, hired 37 new staff members.

At first, the teacher turnover was exciting and the school was filled with a raw energy and enthusiasm that comes with a new team. This new crew of teachers are fully aware of the standards and how to develop aligned lessons with systematic use of assessments. On top of that, their understanding of instructional technology is impressive. They even attend extra-curricular activities for fun! Dr. Collins knew these teachers were skilled technically and he wasn't naive about their lack of real practice. He also had an impression, as his experience held true, that classroom management would be a challenge. He realized, though, that their strengths outweighed their potential weaknesses, so he was excited for this school year. Even though he had 18 new teachers at once, which was about what they were averaging over the last three years, the excitement prevailed over any sense of anxiety about so many new people to supervise.

Now, a third of the way into the school year, Dr. Collins is facing a challenge he didn't expect, which is about the new teachers' ability to cooperate with another and to develop team synergy. Of course, some teachers clicked, but unfortunately that's what developed—clicks. Individually the teachers are strong, but as the principal, Dr. Collins always stressed the power of teamwork and the benefits of collaboration. As a former Triple-A pitcher, he knew the power of strong teams and how *iron sharpens iron* for the betterment of everyone involved. His skills on the mound transferred into sheer will as a classroom teacher and administrator. Unfortunately, he underestimated the work that would be required to develop these new teachers into team players and what it would take for them to understand and appreciate the remaining veteran teachers. He needed them to recognize the need to work with one another for their improved performance and, most importantly, the students.

As the riff among the new teachers grew, they distanced themselves from the veteran teachers, and the veteran teachers didn't mind the space. Those hired over the last years competed with one another in an unhealthy way, creating a palpable pole-positioning effect, and Dr. Collins knew he had to institute specific teacher leadership development to improve the situation. He knew that he wasn't going to be able to manage the dissent by himself. The new teachers weren't learning and growing from the veterans, which is a key professional maturing process that was lacking. Without it, Dr. Collins knew that they wouldn't develop all of the skills necessary to be master teachers in the future. The biggest problem is that teacher leadership was not occurring organically in the departments and the break rooms as it often does. One major issue with that was that four of the five new chairpersons were relatively new teachers themselves. Dr. Collins attempted to persuade some of the veteran teachers to fill the vacancies, but many had held significant roles in the past and wanted to give the new hires the chance to grow and develop as leaders. Typically, this was not even allowed in the contract. Teacher leaders needed to be tenured, but under these circumstances Dr. Collins had no other choice. Knowing that the teacher leaders needed specific leadership development, primarily on teamwork, he designed a leadership curriculum that involved book studies and a series of videos he found online and then vetted to determine if they captured all the ingredients for a successful team.

What is Troubling Dr. Collins?

Dr. Collins quickly realized that the teacher leaders needed strong direction and mentoring. He carved out time within the steering committee meetings and created a teacher leader PLC to develop needed skills, focused on effective collaboration through teamwork. The challenge is that three months into the training, and after reading and discussing the book on highly effective teams, they are not applying the content and the strategies they are learning. In fact, he's afraid that the concepts that they read and discussed are actually reinforcing their bad leadership qualities. The teachers are not seeing how they are contributing to the divide that is occurring among the teaching staff or how they are competing with one another. They are not reading the book through the lens of self-improvement or personal leadership growth, but rather from the perspective that those they lead need to be better followers. Dr. Collins intended for them to see themselves in the characters in the book but instead they're seeing their peers as the characters. The comments from the team demonstrate a lack of self-reflection: "I've tried that but wow, Mr. so-and-so is just stuck in his old ways" or "My team really needs to read this, we would be much better off."

Dr. Collins has attempted to steer the conversation so the participants are more reflective and has asked poignant questions to guide their growth, but he is getting the sense that the very creation of the leadership team development group reinforced the participants' notion that they are superior, uncovering more of the "us" versus "them" mentality that is taking over the staff. The next phase of the session is focused on short video clips from a variety of sources—some funny, a few serious, some from television, a couple from movies, and others from free online sources specifically dealing with teamwork. The videos are between two and five minutes long and touch on very specific themes associated with teamwork.

Leadership Steering Committee Meeting

The steering committee meetings are 60 minutes long, agenda driven, and follow three distinct areas of focus, called the critical three (Figure 7.1):

1. Review and Reflect
2. The Instructional Imperative
3. Leadership Matters

The *Review and Reflect* agenda item is dedicated to taking the time for the team to review the previous and forthcoming months' school-wide events, initiatives, and programs so that they can evaluate whether or not the core work is aligned to the vision of the school. The school has a clear, concise, and powerful vision. This activity ensures that the school's *WHY* is at the forefront of every meeting for extreme focus that drives success (Sinek, 2011). The *Instructional Imperative* agenda item allows the team the time to look at various data points, primarily observation and walkthrough feedback, that is specifically aligned to the school's instructional focus. This year the school embraced six guiding instructional strategies that should be used in every classroom, and the feedback should indicate that. And lastly, the *Leadership*

Figure 7.1 Leadership Team Meeting Agenda

Matters agenda item is geared toward developing the teacher leaders' skills. This is time carved into each meeting where Dr. Collins can grow with and help to grow his key teacher leaders so that their influence is the best it can be.

This month's video clip is from the hit sitcom *The Office*, which is chocked full of mishaps, poor leadership, and bizarre scenarios, which makes it great for learning what not to do as a leader. For this month's steering committee meeting, Dr. Collins chooses a scene where some of the employees feel alienated during Michael's activity. (Michael Scott is the lead character and his role is the Regional Manager of the Scranton branch of the company called Dunder Mifflin, Inc.) The activity is intended to support a cohesive, inclusive, and sensitive work environment, but it utterly fails. The two-minute video is used to springboard the conversation on how to create an environment centered on trust so that the teacher leaders can promote trust among staff members.

How Dr. Collins Actually Conducted the Leadership Steering Committee Meeting

Dr. Collins started the meeting by covering the first two areas, the *Review and Reflect* and the *Instructional Imperative*, and then moved on to the *Leadership Development* portion.

Dr. Collins said, "This month we are continuing with our leadership development, specifically on how to build trust within our teams. To jumpstart our conversation, let's watch a short clip from *The Office*."

The team watched the three-minute clip and then Dr. Collins told them to work with the person next to them in a think–pair–share. To guide the activity, he asked them to think about the video and to consider three major areas when reflecting and answering the associated questions. He distributed the following:

1. The first area of focus is on the *format* of the training in the video and if the activity that Michael uses will likely increase sensitivity among staff members and yield a more trusting work environment.

   (a) What were some of the mistakes Michael made in the training?

   (b) How could he have made the session more effective?

2. The second area of focus is on *employee engagement* and how Michael attempts to involve everyone, essentially coaxing them to behave a certain way.

   (a) What was his method for increased engagement?

   (b) How did his behavior impact the participants?

3. The third area of focus is on the *outcomes of the training*.

   (a) What are some takeaways from the video in terms of what not to do?

   (b) When dealing with sensitive issues or challenging situations, what are some ways to approach them?

After the pairs discussed the questions, Dr. Collins regrouped them and asked them to share some of their thoughts. Mr. Kim, who is in his third year and is currently the social studies chairperson, responded that teambuilding is challenging. He went on to say that with all of our differences, the leader should learn how to build connections. Mrs. Brown, the science chair, responded by saying that, at times, the challenge is that groups of people can be so different and not share the same ideals with one another. The entire group admitted that the video was comical and that Michael makes a lot of mistakes. He very often alienates others versus developing a team mentality. His antics garner him the opposite of his intended purpose. At this, Mr. Tennyson, a veteran teacher within group, added that this is where great leaders can soar, by tapping into the differences that people have and using everyone's strengths as a collective advantage.

Dr. Collins thanked the group and then asked them the final question, "How can we build stronger teams in our respective departments?" Both Mrs. Hall and Mrs. Alistair, the elective and ELA chairs, answered that team-building activities and icebreakers, when done right, are a great way to start meetings and can create a sense of belonging. Mr. Kim added that having clear norms, such as respecting differing opinions and watching how much one person talks, are good strategies to use so that everyone has a chance to participate.

(Continued)

The 20 minutes went by quickly and Dr. Collins closed the meeting by thanking the group and asking them to think about what they discussed and how they can build stronger teams to work toward a culture of trust in their departments. Everyone nodded, and they adjourned.

What Dr. Collins Should Have Done Differently

Dr. Collins has key structures in place for a productive leadership development session. Similar to our other situations, though, there are discrete changes that should be made to have a greater impact so that the teacher leaders are growing. His approach to their development is a common method for professional learning and is often ineffective, yielding 10 percent gains at best. But we do note that it's better than nothing, pausing here to say that some schools don't have leadership teams, those that do don't spend enough time on leadership, and the minority group are the schools with highly effective leadership teams because they have highly effective leadership development strategies. With that said, Dr. Collins' leadership development session lacks a clear focus. Yes, the participants know that they are studying teamwork and learning how to build trust, but there needs to be a distinction between *what* is being studied and *why* it is being studied, which is where the candor is missing in this case.

Although developing leaders is complex, the actual process should be simple. The major shift that Dr. Collins needs to make is in his assumption that covering the material and having great discussions on the topic will somehow lead to growth for the teacher leaders. Leadership development must be intentional with clear outcomes and required actions for the participants. However, too often, when it comes to change and growth for our people, we rely on hope and osmosis, thinking that covering information will be enough since the content is good and the conversations are thought-provoking. Reviewing new ideas, reading leadership books, or attending seminars is only a start to leadership development. Dr. Collins makes this precise mistake, believing that the content will be powerful enough to sink in as if the consumers of it will somehow digest it and understand what it means to take action.

In our example, the conversations are good, but they will remain theoretical and not make their way into daily practices unless the session is viewed through a personal growth lens by the participants. They need to be clear that the area being studied is a specific skill that they need to develop to lead more effectively. When developing specific leadership competencies, it is critical to be direct and let the team know what you are asking them to do things differently, how you've come to this conclusion with evidence, and how you intend to help them and yourself grow for the betterment of the organization. In our scenario, Dr. Collins has an obligation to fix the riff among staff members and bring to light how working in a pole-positioning environment erodes trust. That part of the equation eludes his team altogether, demonstrating the osmosis effect twice: once when he assumes that they know what the problems are and once when he assumes that the readings and videos will be adequate on their own.

How He Could Have Conducted the Steering Committee Meeting with Candor

(Italics represent new/additional text from original statement.)

Dr. Collins started the meeting by covering the first two areas, the *Review and Reflect* and the *Instructional Imperative* and then moved on to the *Leadership Development* portion.

Dr. Collins said, "This month we are continuing with our leadership development, specifically on how to build trust within our teams. *I need to take a moment to clarify why this work is critical for our success and bring to light two issues that we need to be aware of. The first is a potential divide that is occurring among the staff and the second is a competitiveness among some of our teachers that could become unhealthy.*

Let me first address the riff. What I'm noticing is a divide between some of our veteran teachers and the newer staff. I don't want to get mired in finger-pointing or blaming. That's won't help us as leaders. It is vital that we acknowledge issues and work to fix them before they hinder our performance. We will be tackling this together, and we have to grow as leaders if we're going to have a positive influence. The second issue is in drawing a distinction between healthy versus unhealthy competition. Through healthy competition we can sharpen one another and ensure we are all functioning at our best. But, unhealthy competition

(*Continued*)

erodes trust whereby individuals become more important than our school or our vision. Again, we could spend a significant amount of time circling these issues and debating what's going on and why. However, as leaders we have to take responsibility for these situations and work to fix them, regardless of how they started or who was responsible for their inception. So, that is what we are going to do, together.

To jumpstart our conversation, let's watch a short clip from The Office. Please know that even though this is funny and no one on our team operates like Michael, I want you to find opportunities where he could have made a powerful impact. Please reflect on how you can work in your own departments to build trust as we move our school forward as a team. Think about the specific actions that you will take as next steps based on the video and our conversations.

The team watches the three-minute clip and then Dr. Collins tells them to work with the person next to them in a think–pair–share.

Similar to our original scenario, he uses the three major areas as a guide for reflection. Once Dr. Collins brings them back as a whole group, he asks poignant questions to get to the heart of leadership and learning to lead better. Watching and then discussing the film serves as the gateway to the discussion about what really matters, which is what needs to be changed subsequent to the meetings.

Dr. Collins transitions to his direct questions:

Now, let's discuss how you can lead yourself and others? What I am passing out is a sheet with four questions that we are going to focus on for the next month or so.

Questions:

Effective leaders realize the power of relationships in building and sustaining trust.

1. *How are you building relationships in your department?*

2. *How are you creating opportunities for people in your department to contribute so that they feel that they are part of the team?*

3. *Lastly, how are you adding value to them and investing in them as teammates?*

Another area we need to be very mindful of is infighting or what I call pole-positioning. Very often this goes unnoticed because the behavior is subtle and passive. It comes in several forms, excluding others or even an unwillingness to contribute or share. So our question is:

4. *How can we harness the energy and passion that drives us while staying focused on our vision and not ourselves?*

This is not a competition but rather a place where everyone can win. The irony is that we can't do that unless we work as a team.

Let's begin with Mr. Kim and work our way to Mrs. Hall. I want you to tell me the specific actions you plan to take as a leader. We'll start with question #1. Mr. Kim....

The Difference

It is important to note that the way Dr. Collins structures his meetings and his use of videos are good. His issue is not the structure and organization of the meeting. His issue is in making assumptions that the team know what the problems are and why they need to lead better for the sake of the school. There are three primary differences that set the second scenario apart from the first, yielding much different and superior results. First, from the outset of the conversation, Dr. Collins explicitly states what they are going to focus on and why he believes it is necessary. The topic of trust within the context of teamwork is purposeful and something that the teacher leaders need to work on. Effective leaders understand the importance of clarity and purpose in everything they do. Dr. Collins is candid about the problem and why it needs fixing. Second, he clearly communicates their topic in terms of effective leadership. This approach allows him to avoid a conversation on the merits of the topic and if there really is a riff or unhealthy competition. Too often leaders get trapped in conversations about whether or not the problem is real, and candid conversations about the problem get derailed simply because someone disagreed with a thought or an idea. Dr. Collins avoids this trap by painting a picture of what great leaders do and how great leaders keep the vision as the priority, making it more important than any one individual person. This view separates the teacher leaders from the problem itself so that they can objectively view the situation to be an effective part of the solution. In essence, he depersonalizes the problem. Because teacher leaders are in a unique position of influence, but not always authority, a candid learning environment has to be such that it enables them to focus on a problem, grow as leaders, and see themselves as providing the solution, all the while that they are in the ranks of the teaching core. This is why stressing leadership development within the particular problem at hand is so powerful. The mindset isn't us-versus-them or "they" have a problem, but rather an ownership that as leaders it is our responsibility to create a thriving work environment.

Third, after they discuss the video and ask some initial questions that spark a conversation, he asks specific questions directly to the teacher leaders about what they are doing now and what action they will take in the future to build trust. This is where candor and compassion flourish. The questions are not accusatory or negative. They are designed to understand what is being done and where opportunities may lie to improve, which is why being explicit when growing leaders is critical. Constructive criticism is tough to hear and growing can be painful. However, in the right environment, it is through overcoming challenges that leaders truly develop the necessary skills to lead. The

---

Here's a Tip

Develop thoughtful questions ahead of time.
Deep questioning is tough. Not only to generate thoughtful, precise questions, but also the ability to ask them with conviction in the moment. One way to help with this is to develop them ahead of time. Great questions will lead to productive conversations. Dr. Collins has a real opportunity to have an authentic, rich conversation that will help him understand the issues better, what his teacher leaders are actually doing, and the areas where he will need to get more involved. Great questions also quiet the leader and force him to listen. Leaders spend an enormous amount of time talking, directing, and making decisions and deep questioning is a great way to slow that down to gather necessary information and force the leader to listen with sensitive ears.

Candor Cancellation #7—*The Osmosisist*

Leaders can't make assumptions. Dr. Collins makes two fatal assumptions in the first version of the scenario: 1) he assumes that the team knows there's a problem; and 2) he assumes that they're learning to lead better by watching the video. He concludes before they even start the discussion that they'll know, understand, and do through osmosis. He needs to be far more candid in his approach and not leave development to chance. Leaders demonstrate care by being direct with a problem and requiring action to fix it, especially when it comes to developing teacher leaders to manage initiatives and changes to the school environment. You can totally avoid the osmosis effect by being candid upfront and throughout the leadership development sessions you have planned for your team.

---

direct questions also put Dr. Collins in a position to influence his team. The video and the questions are tools to effectively teach. In the first scenario, the video and the questions were used in a general and vague context, and their purpose could easily be missed. This is why so many trainings fail to develop the desired skills. Leaders assume that others will understand the context, importance, and expected outcomes of a growth session, but that's rarely the case. It takes candid and compassionate feedback to drive change.

Scenario Two

Professional Development Experience

Session attendees:

- Mrs. Janice Perry, Principal
- Mrs. Anita Smythe, Social Studies Department Chair
- Mrs. Jane Abernathy, ELA Department Chair
- Mr. Bob Roland, Instructional Technology Coach
- Mr. Jacob Bell, Art Teacher

The Situation

Mrs. Perry is the new principal of Smithfield Senior High School, a medium-size school with 730 students in an urban setting. Smithfield is considered by many to be a good school. Public opinion is favorable, and the superintendent and board of education are pleased with the school's performance on a variety of indicators, including state and federal accountability measures. Staff morale is high among a veteran teaching staff with minimal turnover. Mrs. Perry feels fortunate to be named the new principal after serving seven years as an assistant principal at a neighboring school.

Her approach as the new principal, and as someone new to the district, is to listen, to learn, and then to lead. She knows she has to be patient and take time to truly understand the school, the system, and the district before embarking on change or introducing new ideas. This is seemingly easy to do given Smithfield's success, and it follows the advice of her early mentor who stressed avoiding the two common pitfalls that new administrators make: initiating uninformed change and promoting unnecessary initiatives. Changing or eliminating programs with little or no understanding of their full implications *or* introducing new initiatives without an understanding of their potential impact on the entire school are two mishaps that Mrs. Perry couldn't afford to make. Her mentor was famous for his caution that haste, ambition, and insensitivity are common traits of ineffective leaders, especially early in a new position. He told her to be mindful that she must truly know the school, the people, its needs, and, most importantly, its culture prior to embarking on a new course of action.

This advice was easy for Mrs. Perry to live by given her experience as a career and technical education teacher; she believed in the carpenter's motto: "measure twice, cut once." However, after five months in the position, she is uncovering some areas of real concern. Specifically, after doing months of walkthroughs, she noticed a trend that the teachers don't follow the pacing guides. She knows that she needs to dig into this more, but the biggest telltale is that in the same content areas at the same grade levels, teachers are not aligned with one another. She doesn't expect them to be lockstep, but, specifically in social studies, she noticed that the three U.S. history teachers are all on different topics and teaching different skills. It seems that the teachers are pretty much covering whatever they want and some are clearly teaching topics because they like them, not because of the standards. Lastly, which really surprised her, were the instructional strategies being used. Direct instruction was the dominant method with little or no variation. At first glance, the strategies seemed alright, but after months of walkthroughs, the lack of engagement is evident in many classes. Despite Smithfield's success, there is clearly room to grow, and Mrs. Perry knows that there are groups of students being left behind. The sit-and-get methods of the past are dominating instruction, and that's not what's best for students.

She knows that the teachers could and would argue that the success thus far is due to their current methods and that students are learning what they need to know for the assessments. In fact, they most likely would point out that many students are meeting or exceeding the state standards and district benchmarks. Smithfield is successful in many ways and for many of the students it serves. What they are doing is working for most; however, she believes that through research-based innovative strategies, more students could reach the targets. Mrs. Perry also knows that she is working with a powerful well-liked veteran staff. The teaching core, on average, is in their seventeenth year with the vast majority only ever working at Smithfield, an impressive feat in its own right. Interestingly, the past administration has not enjoyed the same stability. Mrs. Perry is the third principal in six years, and despite the turnover, the school remains successful, which is often attributed to the strength and consistency of the staff. She knows these issues need to be discussed and she has confidence in her ability to engage her teachers in thought-provoking action-oriented discussions. To begin the process, she embarks on a professional development experience on proven, high-leverage instructional strategies that she wants to see all of her teachers using in the future. She plans to address the curriculum concerns later, which is a bigger initiative to handle, important nonetheless, but she needs a few quick wins with the teaching strategies, and she doesn't feel that it will be a big lift. She's more wrong than right about that, but it will come down to how well she uses candor and how clearly she communicates compassion. To make the lift lighter, she recognizes the need to develop her teacher leaders so she introduces a train-the-trainer model.

What is Troubling Mrs. Perry?

Mrs. Perry knew that she needed to address a couple different matters and saw value in introducing professional development around key instructional strategies as an initial step to developing her teacher leaders, harnessing buy-in for her vision to implement proven instructional strategies and giving the leaders the ability to improve their influence. She saw it as high value, low risk, filled with potential. She told herself that with a solid veteran staff, the little adjustments and tweaks that she would like to see to instructional performance should be welcomed and could also be the entry point to more dialogue around curriculum alignment in the future. She wanted the professional development to be something her lead teachers could champion so that it was a place to improve their abilities as leaders, developing their leadership skills to make them more effective teacher leaders. She decided to use a train-the-trainer model, believing that by using her teacher leaders to learn the material first she could create "experts." Her experts would then directly oversee the implementation of the new strategies with an added layer of accountability for everyone. The train-the-trainer model would provide ample opportunity to infuse the necessary leadership development, using scenarios and real experiences to guide conversations about leading better.

At first, the sessions seemed to be going well, but after the third professional development experience, she noticed that the conversations and discussions included an interesting response to the strategies that she hadn't noticed in the first two sessions. No one overtly opposed the strategies or denied their effectiveness. They even seemed to appreciate the idea of the effect sizes associated with certain strategies and were attentive and engaged. What became more and more evident, though, were simple comments, acknowledging the strategy with a statement of affirmation, oddly indicating how the teachers already used the strategies and how well the strategies have worked in their classrooms in the past. Before long, her teacher leaders weren't seeing the PD as an opportunity to change their practices or improve their leadership. Rather, the teacher leaders were endorsing the teaching strategies as common practices and the leadership component as something they already do. The ideas and skills being discussed were being lauded as what they have always done and not something that should lead to change. It puzzled Mrs. Perry to say the least.

Uncertain about the mindset among her teacher leaders, Mrs. Perry actually questioned if the teacher leaders could be reflective enough to see opportunities for growth for themselves and their departments. A critical aspect of the train-the-trainer model was to fully leverage the Professional Learning Communities in each department that met weekly. By design, the teacher leaders were supposed to teach the strategy to their departments in the PLC, and then, using the 60 extra planning minutes provided to them daily, observe the strategies in the classrooms they support. They were then to follow up that week to discuss the strategy in the next PLC to gain feedback and offer suggestions for improvement to reinforce successful implementation. Unfortunately, even after several cycles of PLCs and walkthroughs, Mrs. Perry was not seeing the strategies during her walkthroughs and could not gauge the extent to which the strategies were being taught or reinforced by her teacher leaders. It led her to a leadership team meeting where she needed to address this with the team. The goal was for the teacher leaders to share what they were experiencing in their departments in terms of their influence, and the changes taking place instructionally, during the meetings so that they could learn and grow with one another, but this meeting started with Mrs. Perry interjecting a new conversation about what she was seeing.

How She Actually Conducted the Professional Development Session

Mrs. Perry set aside some time at the beginning of the professional development for her teacher leaders to discuss some of her observations and concerns.

Mrs. Perry: "Before we get started on our instructional strategies for this session, I wanted to take a few minutes and ask each of you how you think the professional development is going. Specifically, I would like your thoughts on the instructional strategies, the extent to which you've been implementing them in your classes so far, how your teachers in your department are doing with them, and if you think they are making an impact on engagement with students. Essentially, are they making a difference? Anita, why don't you begin?"

Anita, a lively teacher with a reputation for being tough and kind-hearted, didn't hesitate. "Thanks Principal Perry, I would love to. I have to admit I was a little hesitant and unsure at first, professional development is not my first love. Don't get me wrong, I love learning and getting better as a leader, but PD often seems contrived and not a good fit for learning new ways to teach. However, I like how this PD is going because it is actually reaffirming much of what

(Continued)

I already do. I can't speak for everyone in my department, but I think many of them use the strategies we've covered so far. I've been able to go into the different classrooms and to date they seem to be going well. Of course, we can tweak some things, but take the graphic organizers for example, we use them quite often in social studies."

At this, Principal Perry, a little disturbed, followed up. "Thanks Anita. Do most of you feel the same way as Anita?" The entire group agreed. Bob, the instructional technology coach, added more, "Actually, I think we may need to consider changing a couple things, such as considering how some of these strategies tie into our instructional technology resources. Especially, if we feel we have this covered; honestly, some of this seems a little redundant, an old hat at this point. If we take the tech-twist to it, we might be doing something different for a change. Although, I do think what we are doing is off to a good start with the staff, but mostly because this stuff isn't new."

Bob's comments unsettled Principal Perry even more because from her perspective the strategies were not being used. She could feel herself getting frustrated. She knew what the primary instructional methods were, that many of their high-need students were being left behind, and that this training would benefit them. She responded, "Bob, I appreciate your thoughts but what makes you say 'old hat' or 'redundant' when it comes to these strategies?" Bob, passionate about instructional technology, retorted, "These strategies are great, but I think most of us have them down pat. Honestly, it's a waste of our time, no offense. What I think we need to do is to train the teachers on how to effectively use technology. That's an area that would be very beneficial, especially since a lot of our tech is underutilized." As Bob finished, a few teachers nodded in agreement and echoed his sentiments.

Mrs. Perry, now quite frustrated and feeling like the meeting was going in a completely different direction, raised her voice a little, shook her head, and responded, "Bob, I have to disagree completely. I am not seeing what any of you are saying. In fact, Anita, I'm not sure how you can even say the strategies are being used at all." Her voice rising even more. "Yes, I believe many of you know these strategies, but they are not being used, and in some cases, they are not being used with precision. In fact, I've been in all of the social studies classes several times each so far this year, and the only time I've seen graphic organizers being used is during movies. Bob, you want to start moving toward using instructional tech to enhance these strategies, but we don't have these down yet. They may be an 'old hat,' but it's not like anyone is wearing it. All I see when I go into classrooms is stand-and-deliver with students barely paying attention. I know many of our students are successful, but I'm not convinced that it's because of the strategies we are using."

With tension increasing in the room and the teachers taken aback by what Principal Perry said, the ELA chair, Jane, spoke up: "I have to admit, Mrs. Perry, your comments seem to be coming out of nowhere. We work incredibly hard, and our students are successful because of us. We know we can improve, which is why we wanted to do the PD, but to suggest that we don't know the strategies or that we are not the reason for the school's success, is simply insulting." "Jane..." interrupted Principal Perry, "I know this is a hard-working staff, I'm not saying that, and I'm not questioning anyone's loyalty or work ethic, but I do believe there is an unrealistic picture of what is actually being done each day in our classrooms. We have more work to do, and it begins with a clear understanding of where we are as a team of instructional leaders."

At this, the room fell silent and the divide was unfortunately clear.

What Mrs. Perry Should Have Done Differently

Developing teacher leaders is challenging, and it requires principals to have a sensitivity to their simultaneous roles as teachers and as leaders. It demands a unique set of skills for teacher leaders to lead their colleagues. Very often they aren't trained or equipped to influence their peers, driving toward a goal that demands change and requires accountability. Mrs. Perry's approach in the use of a train-the-trainer model is a good idea and can work well to develop their leadership skills at the same time as addressing the instructional needs. What she failed to do is to see the big picture from the teacher leaders' perspective and address their leadership development needs as they work to practice them during the PD. She became mired in what she thought was the problem—their inability to be reflective on their teaching practices and their lack of desire to change. She formed judgments on her thoughts, she didn't ask direct questions about the leadership experiences, and she failed to empathize with them. She simply missed an opportunity to grow the leaders, and the irony is that she tried to take a softer angle when she opened the meeting with the questions.

She didn't recognize or consider that they may be afraid to violate their colleagues' trust or that they may be uncomfortable with holding them accountable. What she perceived as an unwillingness to be reflective, and a lack of honesty about their performance, was based on her assumptions and not a full understanding of her teacher leaders and their skills. Consider Bob's comments about a different focus. Mrs. Perry thought he was simply disregarding the initiative. Although that may be the case, it doesn't have to be. One of the biggest mistakes leaders make is in not seeking to fully understand why something is being said and why someone feels a certain way. Bob may simply know that the teachers aren't that good with the technology, and it would be an easier "sell" for him and the others to introduce the strategies from that lens. Bob may actually be getting push back from his colleagues about planning to use the technology resources, and Mrs. Perry doesn't fully listen with a desire to understand why Bob claims that they should go in a different direction. She falls into the common trap of only hearing things that reinforce her thoughts and ideas.

Another shift Mrs. Perry can make is with her level of questioning. We touched on this in the last scenario with Dr. Collins. Deep thoughtful questioning takes time and should clearly seek the desired answers. Instead, Mrs. Perry asked the following questions all at once and in succession:

1. What are your thoughts on the instructional strategies?
2. To what extent have you been implementing them in your classes?
3. How are your teachers in your department are doing?
4. And do you think they are making an impact and engaging more students in your class?

Because she asks these questions in an informal, broad, and generic manner, it sets the tone for the meeting where anyone can make general claims about the success or failure of the initiative so far. Rather than establishing the need for concrete answers on the progress of the initiative, she inadvertently establishes a loose conversational approach to simply gather more information. However, since she already believes that there is little change, and that the strategies are not being supported, her line of questioning is actually passive aggressive. Her questions don't capture the essence of what she wants them to actually reflect on. As a result, she gets upset when the conversation goes in a totally different direction, and she feels they aren't being reflective or willing to change. This is where candor and compassion can be used effectively. Compassion demands a sensitivity to the people and the situation. Mrs. Perry needed to gather more information about their leadership before she has them reflect on the practices. Is it that the leaders don't know the strategies themselves or is it is that they don't want to push their peers? Knowing this allows Mrs. Perry to get answers about what's bothering her without making unnecessary and disastrous assumptions. Additionally, it would have been better to be candid about what she is and isn't seeing and use that for conversation and leadership development. The more direct position may create similar tension but without the flare that ensued based on the impression that the teachers have that everything is going fine when it's not. If she wants the answers to the four questions, she should save that for later in the meeting. Rather, she should open with very direct statements and work on the team's ability to lead first, before entering into the conversation about the strategies. The teaching strategies will always follow the teacher leaders' ability to lead others to use them and never the other way around.

How She Should Have Conducted the Professional Development Session with Candor

(Italics represent new/additional text from original statement.)

Mrs. Perry set aside some time in the beginning of the professional development to discuss some of her observations and concerns.

Mrs. Perry: "Before we get started on our instructional strategies for this session, I want to take a few minutes to *discuss the professional development. I first want to share my findings so far from my*

(Continued)

walkthroughs and then I want to get your perspective. Please keep in mind that this initiative is about two things: teaching strategies and your leadership development.

As you know, I conduct walkthroughs each day with the expectation that the strategies we are focusing on are being implemented. I believe in the train-the-trainer model for many reasons, but particularly with each of you because of your relationship with your colleagues and the belief I have in each of you as leaders. The areas I want to discuss and focus on are based on what I am not seeing in the classrooms. That being said, you have the direct relationships with your team and are working with them on a daily basis so I wanted to understand your perspective, to equip you with the necessary tools, and to make sure we are all clear on the expectations moving forward. To be explicit, I am not seeing a change in our instructional practices, and for us to be an effective leadership team, we have to be on the same page. Please help me to understand your perspective.

Let's begin, first, with a reflection about your role in this initiative as a teacher leader and any complications or challenges you're are experiencing with this. Include in your reflection an assessment of the consistent and pervasive use of our strategies in your specific department."

Providing Anita still disagrees and uses the graphic organizer example, Mrs. Perry can respond with the following, *"Thank you Anita. Can you please give me specific examples from your walkthroughs that lead you to believe these are being implemented with precision? To date, I've conducted several walkthroughs in each of the classrooms in the social studies department, and I have not seen them being used. If I'm frank here, the only places I am seeing use of graphic organizers is when we're showing films. The goal is for these strategies to be consistent and pervasive as we discussed. Moving forward, please let me know when you and others will be using the strategies so that I can see them in action."*

Let's get back to our reflection on the train-the-trainer model and how the PLCs are going. As we reflect on our leadership and influence in our departments regarding the strategy implementation, we can help one another grow as leaders. Jane, how are the PLCs going with the ELA department?

The Difference

It is quite possible that even if Mrs. Perry opens with her candid position about the strategies, she still may get pushback, specifically from Anita. Anita may argue that they are seeing the effective use of graphic organizers, reaffirming that what they are doing is tied to the initiative. The goal of candor isn't to control what people say, stifle their thoughts, or allow the leader to direct the outcome of the meeting. Actually, it is the complete opposite. Candor allows for open and honest dialogue on a clear and specific topic. If Mrs. Perry disagrees with Anita's assessment of her team's progress, she can then be direct and provide evidence as to why she disagrees, such as her walkthrough and observation data. Doing so re-establishes the goals of the meeting. This won't necessarily change Anita's mind, but it does set the appropriate stage for Mrs. Perry to identify what is expected with clear next steps. By opening with what she is not seeing, she prevents herself from getting frustrated when she hears the opposite of what she's thinking. She flips the scenario entirely, giving feedback first before the reflection activity.

The goal of the meeting, at least the start of it, was to uncover the reasons why the initiative is failing and to assess the teacher leaders' effectiveness in supporting the changes. In the first version of the scenario, Mrs. Perry appears to bate the team with questions about the use of the strategies that she already knows the answer to, and then she's frustrated by the responses. The team needs candid feedback from a patient leader, and that's what we get in the second version. Mrs. Perry, instead, designed the meeting to uncover the reality of the situation and truly seek perspective so that the team can learn from one another. Interestingly, the second version is still slightly tense. There is still disagreement, but disagreements can be handled professionally. Regardless of how Anita responds, the next step is still to understand—either she doesn't know the strategies well enough herself or she isn't pushing her department. Consider if Anita agreed with Mrs. Perry and simply stated that she's not challenging her teachers because they are not receptive and they don't see the relevance. That admission would open the door for Mrs. Perry to take the next steps to help lead Anita and equip her to develop the necessary skills to support the initiative and hold her teachers accountable. This is why clear feedback is critical to teacher leader development. The entire tone of the meeting goes from passive-aggressive questioning and then opposition to fully candid feedback and a reflection on the challenges of leadership. The likely outcome of the second version is a realization that the team needs to have more influence, creating space to discuss scenarios to learn to lead better as teachers.

Here's a Tip

Formally assess your team's strengths and weaknesses.
Leaders sometimes introduce methods and strategies that should allow for leadership development experiences without truly knowing if they will work with their staff members. Train-the-trainer is a great model for leaders to learn and then demonstrate expertise for influence; however, when using it with a team, the leader must be certain that the trainers are equipped to deal with all the challenges they will face. Many individuals who possess the technical skills associated with the strategy are not necessarily equipped to train others. They simply may lack the skills to train their peers effectively or the influence it takes to garner subsequent application. Mrs. Perry chose the strategy because she thought it would be useful, and she wanted to capitalize on the teachers' solidarity and camaraderie. That's a great idea, but it's only one piece of the puzzle. The other piece is that the team has to have the skills to lead the initiative. This is actually a critical aspect of candor that Mrs. Perry could have used in the very beginning to determine if they were ready to lead the initiative. She jumps to a question about how the strategies are being used when she needs them to reflect on their leadership roles.

Candor Cancellation #8—*The Easer Inner*

Never ease into a difficult conversation. Beating around the bush or trying to bait someone into an admission doesn't work. Mrs. Perry tried to ease in when she needed to be candid about the problem and then develop her teacher leaders to be able to solve it. She tried to set up a situation and then she lost control. Because of this, the meeting simply ended, providing everyone with an out in the situation.

When the leader doesn't address a problem head-on, or, worse, loses control, future accountability becomes nearly impossible. The better angle to take is to provide evidence, face the facts, and clarify expectations for the team. Easing in only cancels the leader's ability to be candid later because doing so demonstrates that the leader was trying to be disingenuous with a soft attempt to fix a hard problem.

Scenario Three

Face-to-Face Coaching

Principal: Dr. Ed Rodriguez
　　Leadership team member:

- Mr. Simon James, Mathematics

The Situation

In a previous scenario we met Principal Rodriguez who embarked on an aggressive instructional technology campaign at Marshall T. High School. When we met Dr. Rodriguez, he was attempting to use a collaborative leadership model to advance the initiative, considering that it was not progressing, and he was at a loss as to how to move it forward. We dissected his approach and identified that the primary issue was not holding his teacher leaders accountable for their role in the plan to be sure that the technology was being implemented appropriately. Furthermore, he continued to simply revisit the implementation of the plan and never dealt with the real issues behind the plan not working. When we exhibited the candid version of the scenario, his approach improved and so did his success.

The great news for Dr. Rodriguez, his teachers, and, most importantly, the students of MTHS is that now six months later the initiative is progressing well. His new approach to using the department heads differently and adding layers of accountability is working. The challenge now is that the progress within each department is not consistent. Dr. Rodriguez quickly realized that not all department teacher leaders possess the same skills and strengths. Applying what he learned from his collaborative decision mistake, and the need to specifically hone in and target the real issues at hand, he instituted face-to-face coaching sessions to specifically develop each teacher leader. He recognized that each person was unique with vastly different skill sets. The sessions were time consuming, but the individual growth among the teacher leaders was amazing.

Each department head was responsible for the implementation of the instructional technology initiative in their respective department. Since this work was outlined and detailed in the steering committee meetings, they were clear on what the initiative looked like in each area and were able to use department meeting time to reinforce expectations, support implementation, and troubleshoot any complications. Once those three areas were covered, similar to Maslow's hierarchy of needs, the expectations and use of the technology grew, particularly with sophistication. For example, in world language they started employing an app to reinforce language acquisition in a blended learning environment. The students watched videos designed by the teachers to reinforce concepts taught during the class, and the app capitalized on basic language retrieval in various contexts to boost the students' vocabulary acquisition. At the start, this was a massive undertaking, but the teachers embraced the charge and even first-year language learners were progressing faster than ever before according to their common proficiency assessments.

The reality, though, was that not every department had the same desire to pursue these alternative educational methods, and some department leaders were ill equipped to both support and challenge their staff. They seemed to have one or the other, but not both together. Mr. James, the math chair, definitely fell into the support category, but he lacked the skill to challenge his team with high expectations. The department was not implementing the ideas, and, as such, they were lagging behind. As time passed, the gaps grew between the math department's implementation of the technology resources and every other department in the school.

What is Troubling Dr. Rodriguez?

Change takes time and Dr. Rodriguez embraced the fact that the technology initiative is really a major shift in practice and mindset. True cultural changes don't advance quickly. His expectations are realistic, yet aggressive. Once the departments were clear on how to use the technology, what changes were expected, and what it actually looked like in classrooms, many of the departments evolved rapidly. Unfortunately, the math department is lagging behind under the direction of Mr. James, the department head, and changes to instructional practices are minimal. The use of the technology in the mathematics classrooms is sporadic at best.

Dr. Rodriguez's face-to-face coaching with Mr. James is very explicit, and they meet frequently. Mr. James is not only quite knowledgeable in the use of the technology himself and supportive of his colleagues, he is also very receptive to the coaching. He desires to grow as a leader, but, to date, the math department is not using the two primary instructional technology tools that go hand-in-hand with the electronic whiteboard. The first is an online interactive formative assessment program that allows the teachers to design assignments that engage students in a step-by-step fashion so that the teacher can monitor students from a central computer. With it, teachers are given the capability of monitoring student progress in real time, all at once, and can immediately intervene as they see fit.

Because many of the ninth grade students are lacking the necessary algebra skills, this tool was identified as a great way to inform teachers so that they can make the decision to reteach, remediate, or scaffold. Initially, the teachers had to recreate all of the assignments within the online platform, but once this is done, maintenance and improvements are relatively easy. However, there is not a consistent effort to build the assignments, and, hence, the tool is not being used effectively or consistently in the department.

The second major push was similar to that in the world language department, and focused on word choice and language acquisition. Many students simply do not understand the vocabulary associated with the math problems. The teachers identified that some of the gaps in learning occur due to the confusion students are having in regard to certain terms and processes that appear on the assessments. The questions use vocabulary that is foreign to the students, and they do not know or understand what the question is actually asking. Knowing that this is an issue that could be readily fixed, the teachers were charged with using the learning management system to build support activities for key vocabulary with sample questions and accompanying videos for each of the units within the courses. However, little has been done to accomplish this task. The online platform was organized to get them started, but the portal is mostly empty.

Originally, the teachers agreed that these were necessary areas of focus, and they had exemplars to guide the creation process. Mr. James set out to use the PLC time to outline the scope of work and establish teams with "project managers" to facilitate each step. Yet, despite his organization, leading by example, and pleas to his department, Mr. James cannot bring everything and everyone together. Teachers miss deadlines on content creation, they don't try to use what does exist, and they are in many ways passive aggressive toward the initiative. Dr. Rodriguez is beginning to wonder if Mr. James, despite being an incredibly skilled teacher, has the capability and capacity to lead his department, even with the supports he has from his leadership teammates and the principal.

How He Actually Conducted the Face-To-Face Meeting

The face-to-face meetings take place in the principal's office.

Dr. Rodriguez:

"Simon, I want to begin our coaching session by recapping our goals from the last meeting, discussing your progress to date, and then covering the leadership skill that we focused on to support your work. We established two primary goals: the first one was for you to identify and recruit a key person as the lead within each math section, such as Algebra I, to help you create the content for their particular section. That person would serve as the primary contact to report on progress and give you updates and feedback. The second goal was to build the first unit for each section in both the online interactive program and the learning management system. Considering each math section has at least three teachers, we both felt that this approach would work. We also know that, although your team seems supportive, the work is not getting done. As a result, we spent significant time talking about how you can use a pressure/support model to hold your team accountable. I can't wait to hear your progress, so let's start with your goals."

At this point, Simon shifted in his seat and started with good news. "Ok, we have definitely made progress. Judith said that she will be the lead for Algebra, John will take Geometry, and I am still working on the others, but having two committed, I thought, was a pretty good step. Regarding actual development, we got some ideas out on the table during our PLC, and I thought we had a decent sketch laid out, but unfortunately we haven't built the content. I know we wanted the first unit done by now, so we are a little behind, but I'm confident we will have it done within the next two weeks before our next session. I spoke to Judith and John, and I think we are good to start working."

Dr. Rodriguez, knowing that Simon is struggling with being direct with his team, eased into the next part of the conversation. "Simon, I do want to say that you possess two great leadership qualities. You lead by example, and you have passion. But, as you know, we've also talked about your ability to motivate your team so that they are also doing their part. This is a concern of mine. I will do all I can to support you, but as the teacher leader in the math department, I need you to facilitate this work with your teachers. Walk me through why you could only get two commitments and why there is no content developed thus far."

Simon cleared his throat and started with some general obstacles. "Ed (Dr. Rodriguez), you know that this is a tough time of year for the math department. Our last meeting got bogged down with the upcoming state assessment and the next thing I knew ... our time was done. I am also confident that I can get Jane to be the lead for the upper level math courses. She was hesitant when I asked her, but I think she will come around." At this, Ed politely interrupted, "Simon, I realize there is a lot of pressure on the math department and that our state test is right around the corner. Honestly, that's why this work is so pressing, to really help remediate and hone in on our students' needs, and we are already lagging behind. I feel like we continue to circle these issues on your meetings getting derailed and a lack of commitment from your team members. Did you use the active meeting strategies that we covered last time in our face-to-face?"

Simon simply reverted back to how the meeting was consumed by the upcoming assessments. "Ed, I really tried to use the strategies, the agenda was set, I went over our goals, and then Bill asked if he

(Continued)

could pose a question before we got started. The next thing I knew, we were in a heavy conversation on the assessments. I know we didn't make the necessary progress, but it was a good conversation that dealt with many of our concerns. I feel like we covered a lot of ground. For our next meeting, we all committed to hitting the ground running and working on the platform." Even as Simon wrapped up his response, he was starting to feel uncomfortable. He knows he is struggling with the initiative, so rather than hearing Dr. Rodriguez's reply, he finished by asking for more time, and he really reassured Dr. Rodriguez that his team was turning the corner to getting the units built.

As Simon finished talking, Dr. Rodriguez was at an impasse. The truth is that he likes Simon as a person and respects him greatly as a teacher. Furthermore, no one in the math department has his instructional technology capability or even the rapport that he has with students. As a result, he encouraged him, reminded him of the importance of the goals, thanked him for his time, and ended the meeting by setting the same goals from the previous face-to-face coaching session for the next one in a few weeks.

What Dr. Rodriguez Should Have Done Differently

Our scenarios with Dr. Rodriguez, whether it is collaborative decision-making or his use of teacher leaders, both highlight the challenges associated with change initiatives in schools. Larger initiatives that reshape a school or district's culture require everyone to have the stamina and desire to achieve the results because each step along the way potentially houses a challenge, small or large, that can halt or completely derail the efforts. Dr. Rodriguez's technology initiative is experiencing the issues and challenges often associated with new expectations that require staff to make changes to their practices, put in extra time, and stay true to the belief that all of their effort will pay off in the end. Time, depending on the scenario, can be a leader's best friend or worst foe. Simon James, the math chair, is hitting roadblock after roadblock with his staff, and despite his own talent and optimism, the department is falling further and further behind in their own timeline while the other departments in the school move forward.

We find Dr. Rodriguez in a face-to face coaching session with Mr. James. There is incredible power and potential when a leader directly mentors someone and provides them with the essential tools necessary for success. Like all of our other scenarios, there is a major error made by Dr. Rodriguez in this face-to face development session, and it's all too common. Face-to-face coaching is a two-sided coin. On the one side there is what needs to be taught. This is pre-planned information, ideas, and skills to teach and develop the individual. Herein lies part of the power of direct interaction. On the other side of the coin is the information that the individual brings to the coaching session, which is his personal experiences. For coaching sessions to be valuable, the leader must be a master of both sides, teaching the necessary skills and capitalizing on the experiences as learning opportunities. It is within these personal experiences that a person has emotional attachment, opinions, and records of how they handled past situations. Powerful sessions use this side of the coin to reinforce ideas and introduce new skills that enhance the person's leadership abilities.

Face-to-face coaching, or any other situation we've presented, is not conducted in a vacuum without the many related variables. One unique and unpredictable aspect of coaching is the information that the coach receives from the individual being coached. A skilled leader knows how to listen to what is being said and adapt his message to lead the other person. Although it sounds like a simple play on words, the difference is the intent and outcomes of the session when it is treated as a *debrief* versus a *report out*. A debrief, as we define it within the context of face-to face coaching, is an interactive process used to assess the situation, to evaluate the people involved, and to offer feedback and guidance to improve the situation and the individual's performance for another upcoming experience. In our scenario, Dr. Rodriguez treats this part of the session more like a report out, which doesn't have the same expectations for the individual giving the information. Reporting out is not an interactive, growth-oriented process. Rather, it is generally one-sided with one person reporting and another person passively receiving information. Dr. Rodriguez does go back and forth somewhat with Mr. James, but stops short of truly evaluating his performance with feedback and direction for him to take several crucial next steps.

It is important to note that the session does include some positive elements, such as a clear focus, identified goals, a specific timeline, and direct questioning. His issue is not the structure of the meeting. It is his willingness to be direct with Mr. James's skill level as a teacher leader.

At some point, Dr. Rodriguez must evaluate Mr. James and comment on more than just the situation. Debriefing allows for that to occur. The meeting should not have ended by pushing deadlines back and hoping that Mr. James will be successful at a later date. The meeting should uncover why Mr. James is unable to get his team on track to achieve the objectives that they set. Dr. Rodriguez already mentored him on active meeting strategies, asks him about it, and yet his answer is vague, demonstrating that the strategies didn't work. The question is why didn't they work? This is a difficult question to ask because it may lead to a difficult decision. It's why candor is often avoided. Dr. Rodriguez may fear the fact that he needs to make a decision about Mr. James as his math department head, whether or not he can get him to a place where he has the ability to lead his team, or if he needs to select a different person altogether. Candid and compassionate feedback will bring these answers to light, allowing leaders to address specific deficiencies or determine if a hiring decision needs to be made.

How He Should Have Conducted the Face-To-Face Meeting with Candor

(Italics represent new/additional text from original statement.)

The face-to-face meetings takes place in the principal's office.

Dr. Rodriguez:

"Simon, I want to begin our coaching session by recapping our goals from the last meeting, discussing your progress to date, and then covering the leadership skill that we focused on to support your work."

This introduction, with a focus on the established goals and a clear agenda, is a great start to the meeting. In the first version of the scenario, Dr. Rodriguez then recaps the goals and touches on the heart of the coaching session, which is on Simon holding his team accountable. He goes on to say, "As a result, we spent significant time talking about how you can use a pressure/support model to hold your team accountable. I can't wait to hear your progress, so let's start with your goals."

As you read, Simon details his progress and also mentions what did not occur so far. The key question that Dr. Rodriguez asks, and needs to dig into further using candor, is, "Did you use the active meeting strategies that we covered last time in our face-to-face?" Simon didn't answer the question directly, rather he mentioned that the assessments conversation ate up all of the time at the PLC, and he made an excuse with, "Ed, I really tried to use the strategies, the agenda was set, I went over our goals, and then Bill asked if he could pose a question before we got started. The next thing I knew, we were in a heavy conversation on the assessments." Simon continues in this manner and then reassures Dr. Rodriguez that they will get the work done. This is the pivotal part in the conversation and where candor is missing. Dr. Rodriguez starts out really well, and uses proven meeting techniques, however, it is within the dialogue regarding the progress to date where he falls short, avoiding the major issue at hand.

To make the meeting productive and not just informative, he needs to press further. *"Simon, I can appreciate different agenda items coming up and how the team has other pressing issues. However, we discussed last meeting that one of the key active meeting strategies is to place these popcorn ideas into an established parking lot so the meeting can follow the predetermined agenda. Did you try the parking lot strategy with Bill's question on assessments?"*

Regardless of Simon's response, whether he did try or did not, the reality is that he was unable to redirect Bill for some reason. Additional questions should be designed to gather more information on the situation to help guide Dr. Rodriguez's next steps with Simon. For our scenario, we will assume that Simon did try to stick to the agenda. Simon responds to Dr. Rodriguez, *"Of course, I tried, but Bill asked if he could pose the one question and then I did attempt to place it on the parking lot poster paper, but then someone else spoke up, and before I knew it I was fielding several questions."* Knowing this can be a common pattern in meetings, Dr. Rodriguez responds, *"Simon, I appreciate your being forthright with me. The challenge that I am facing with this is that in terms of importance right now for*

(Continued)

the students, the technology goals currently outweigh the assessment issues. The agenda should have been followed, and if there was any time left over, then assessments could have been discussed. During our last coaching session, we discussed your ability to redirect and keep your meetings focused. We examined other forms of communication to discuss concerns of this kind. For example, we talked about you asking for issues to be sent throughout the week so that PLC time could truly be spent on instruction. Did any of your team members send you items ahead of time that they wanted to talk about?" Simon responded that no one emailed or talked to him about any concerns.

With this information, Dr. Rodriguez responded, "Simon, I have to be straight with you. This position as teacher leader is critical. One important element of the role is that you serve as a conduit of information from the administration to your team and from your team to the administration. Unfortunately, the communication from your department is only one-sided. You are only hearing their concerns and not driving change. We knew you had some roadblocks ahead, but despite our coaching sessions, I am not seeing the necessary changes in your department and, as tough as this is to say, your leadership. You are an excellent teacher and incredibly progressive; yet, I need someone who can also champion the work that needs to get done, rally his team, and accomplish great things, while addressing their concerns and meeting their needs. That is the whole philosophy behind the pressure and support model we have been reviewing. For the remainder of our meeting, I want to go over the active meeting strategies, step-by step, and identify precisely how you could have used them during the meeting in a successful way. I also want to strategize about how you can meet the goals we've identified to get us caught up and establish some other new targets with the technology platform. I know this is a tall order, but we are already behind. Lastly, I want to be fair to you and also very clear, if you can't successfully fill this role and achieve these objectives, we will need to go in another direction with the department, finding someone else to lead it. I only say so now, because at this point, although I will fully support your efforts to turn this around, we have been going in circles with coming back to the same point over-and-over."

The Difference

The second scenario moves beyond *what* occurred to *why* it occurred. To do so, both Dr. Rodriguez and Mr. James need to work in an environment of trust, where sharing ideas and experiences is paramount to understanding the people with whom you work. Being straightforward and direct doesn't necessarily mean the person receiving the message understands it or knows how to take action. For the coaching sessions to be effective, Mr. James must be receptive and open to what Dr. Rodriguez is teaching him, as well as reflective on his own performance. The situation, like many, requires vulnerability for the leadership development to be meaningful for Mr. James. That's where trust is key. However, the coach, in this instance Dr. Rodriguez, is responsible for creating that environment. In both versions of the scenario, Mr. James reassures Dr. Rodriguez that they will be fine without truly reflecting on how bad things have gotten with the management of the technology and his management of the meetings. Typically, this is a defense mechanism whereby Mr. James is working to move past the upcoming difficult conversation as quickly as possible. In the first version, it works and Dr. Rodriguez avoids the issue, allowing it to push to the next meeting. But in the second version, Dr. Rodriguez doesn't avoid the problem. He tackles

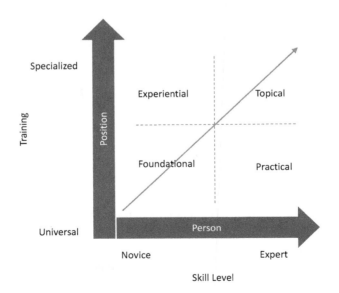

Figure 7.2 Professional Development Continuum

Here's a Tip

Differentiate leadership training.
Developing leaders is a challenge. Great administrators know where their people are on the leadership development continuum, and they tailor professional development accordingly. Unfortunately, the idea of growth is often nebulous. It's reduced to traits and skills that are critical to be an effective leader, but are not always organized and taught in a systematic fashion. As a result, many individuals never fully develop into great leaders. When developing teacher leaders, it is vital to identify the proven leadership qualities and skills that each person must possess, evaluate their levels in each area, and then tailor their leadership development. This process identifies the differences between a beginner, intermediate, and expert level and allows for competency development to occur on a continuum. Great leaders differentiate leadership development to target the specific needs of the people who they are mentoring. General leadership training is fine in the beginning for a novice leader to build a foundation, but as the individual learns and grows, she needs refined teaching to hone and sharpen specific skills (Figure 7.2).

Candor Cancellation #9—*The Avoider*

Don't be a leader who avoids problems. Leadership requires a voice, and when we keep quiet or allow others to silence an issue, we concede to a continuation of the issue. In fact, when leaders avoid concerns, they are communicating that they don't really care about it. That's the opposite of leading with compassionate feedback. Avoidance is the ultimate candor cancellation because it demonstrates that whatever excuses we've made or blame we've placed about not getting results is acceptable. Mr. James blames his team for derailing the momentum they need with the technology integration, and in the first version of the scenario, Dr. Rodriguez allows for it; the simple difference is that in the second version he does not.

it head-on, using Mr. James' communicated experiences at his meeting to dissect the issue and candidly express the next steps.

We end this final scenario with the possibility that Mr. James will be removed from his position. Unfortunately, not all situations end with a glowing resolution. These situations are difficult and should be approached delicately but also directly. Consider a conversation with a doctor, the more serious a situation is for a patient, the more prescriptive the approach needs to be. A doctor doesn't shy away from informing the patient of a severe diagnosis. That would be malpractice. In this same way, employees should always know how well they are performing. The second version of this scenario actually demonstrates more care for the individual than the first. When the leader determines that coaching and support will no longer work, the best decision for everyone is to communicate the intention to remove the person and then follow through.

Conclusion

Great principals rely on strong teacher leaders to create successful learning environments for students. The constant demands on schools require principals to create systems that distribute leadership, responsibility, and accountability throughout the organization. Strong teacher leaders serve as the conduit between the administration and the teaching core. Successful teacher leaders are skilled at vertical two-way communication between their respective departments and the administration, as well as horizontal communication among the staff members in their departments.

Our scenarios highlight common teacher leader development issues for the principal and the teacher leaders. Each situation also has multiple layers that represent common issues found in any given school that require delicate yet candid approaches in order to grow and develop the individuals as leaders.

Our scenarios cover three typical, but often overlooked, teacher leader development pitfalls that leaders find themselves in—*The What, The Out,* and *The Blame.* This will always be the case when leaders cancel candor by being The Osmosisist, The Easer Inner, or The Avoider. The first pitfall is The What—hoping that people will learn to lead without taking real action toward their development. The Osmosisist doesn't identify the actions necessary for change. Dr. Collins found himself without the necessary constructs around the resources used for teaching leadership to his team, hoping that the books, watching videos, and so on will lead to leadership growth. The problem is that people need guidance and clarity on what specific qualities and skills they should focus on for development. The resources that Dr. Collins used are good. It is how he is using them to teach that needs to be improved. Leaders cannot be satisfied with just the act of doing something versus identifying and measuring the desired outcomes. Focusing on the outcomes requires candor and feedback to hold the entire group accountable. The second pitfall is The Out where we see The Easer Inner at work—a leader attempting to ease into difficult conversations or even confront what they are thinking using a vague and broad approach. We contend that this style is misguided since the leader has something specific to discuss but is attempting to steer the conversation in a certain way, working to trick the people into thinking something versus being candid upfront. The false belief in this case is that coming right out and saying something may be too direct, offensive, or offputting. This results in an attempt to ease into difficult conversations but, in fact, it is disingenuous and leads to frustration and distrust. Leaders must be transparent, clear, and candid. The third pitfall is The Blame—a leader not following up to ensure clarity on a particular situation, avoiding it altogether, or skirting around it. Leaders can't let excuses prevail or allow others to blame the team for their shortcomings and lack of performance. When Mr. James blames his department for getting off task, his principal has to bring that back to his ability to lead a focused meeting. Following up, asking numerous questions to gain greater clarity, is critical for tactical decision-making.

All three pitfalls, as described in our scenarios, are common and are clear examples of the lack of candor we experience in schools. Our principals in the scenarios are committed to leading effectively and developing teacher leaders, yet they make simple errors that limit the effectiveness of their feedback. The tips in each section are easy guides to put in place while developing teacher leaders for growth and prosperity with your team.

Conclusion
Outside of the Circle

Being trapped in the circle of nice is a result of fear. We fear that our words and attempts at improving others will damage our relationships and disrupt our own well-being, so we withhold, suppress, and disguise our realities with niceness and ambiguity. We become trapped in the circle of nice, and it thwarts any forward movement in our schools. This doesn't have to be the case, and leaders can take the necessary steps to move outside the circle and into a place where candor and compassion are the norm. When leaders bravely step outside the circle, they can realize new and different results by truly evaluating progress and confronting the reality of the current instructional program, the need for candor at meetings, and whether or not our teachers are truly leading or passively engaged. Candor is not one person's responsibility. Candor and compassion are qualities that create the right environment for leadership to thrive in a growth-oriented space. This type of culture requires deliberate practice to establish and simply will not happen without purposeful actions.

The primary focus of this book is on the technical expertise that leaders need to be able to communicate effective feedback, whether you're giving feedback to teachers in a walkthrough, providing feedback in meetings as you collaborate on decisions, or giving feedback to your teacher leaders. We wanted to demonstrate the importance of giving candid feedback and show the distinct differences between vague and ambiguous feedback compared to candid and specific feedback. The latter is simply more effective and when done well demonstrates respect and care for individuals and the organization. We know from experience that the "best practices" that are touted as successful school-based change initiatives won't work without a candid and compassionate leader. Just doing walkthroughs, implementing collaborative decision-making, or creating teacher leadership positions will have very little impact on school improvement and student success if the leader doesn't ensure that the strategies are implemented and maximized with fidelity, which demands a culture of candor. This requires a skillful leader to create a culture of open-communication between the leader and her team that embraces candid feedback to learn and grow in order to be successful. That's the bottom line and the clear message that we want you to get from this book. But, the greater context of this work is about leadership itself, and, furthermore, accountability in schools.

The first layer of accountability that we hope you take away from this book is that it is the principal who must accept responsibility for all three of the best practices we discussed herein and the outcomes associated with them. That might seem obvious, but it's far more complex in practice than it is in the theoretical sense of the notion. Let's take, for example, conducting instructional rounds and using walkthroughs to give informal feedback to teachers. The literature is clear that these strategies work to improve instructional practices and school culture in general. But, the efficacy of the practice depends upon frequent visits to classrooms with quality feedback to teachers, and we have found in many circumstances that either frequency or quality is missing in the equation. Unless the walkthrough is a major priority at the school level, or it is a district-wide mandate from the central office with a clear support structure, it usually goes on the backburner to those things that administrators need to accomplish in their busy day. In this book, we argue that not only does it need to be at the forefront of our day—visiting classrooms and providing feedback—it must be coupled with candid and compassionate feedback to be effective. We're hoping that this work will inspire principals to hold themselves accountable to doing walkthroughs, visiting classrooms daily, and providing teachers with candid feedback so that they can achieve the results they desire. The same goes for the other two best practices. Unless we're accountable for collaborative decision-making and growing teacher leaders, we'll fall short of excellence in schools.

The second layer of accountability that we hope you'll find as inspiration from this work is a shift in the conversation about teacher and school accountability from standardized test scores to best practices and feedback. You'll get no argument from us about the validity of using standardized tests to measure teacher and school effectiveness. In our time as practitioners, we've seen the standards get clearer and the tests gets better.

We've also witnessed great teaching in practice and watched our best teachers garner the greatest outcomes in terms of student performance. We can go into five rooms and rank order the teaching effectiveness, test the students from those rooms, and literally get the same ranking. But, that's why we want to shift the conversation. The current system of accountability is still an outside-in, external force, that created a culture about just getting results, and the pendulum has swung too far in that direction. It's somehow all about the outcomes, and the output, which overlooks the true nature of success, an intrinsic desire to achieve a worthwhile goal. We contend that test score accountability measures should be a byproduct of the vision with a clear focus on the inputs that lead to achievement and success. Schools, principals, and teachers should be accountable for the way in which they do business, not just their scores. In fact, we believe this is what most educators desire for themselves and their colleagues, a level of professionalism that holds them to a standard of excellence with using best practices every day. For classroom teachers, that means using the most effective teaching strategies to reach every child. For principals, it means developing a culture where candid and compassionate feedback is expected from everyone in all situations for the betterment of the students, the school, and ultimately the community.

A transformation will occur if we quit relying on outside measures and test scores to understand our practices and start talking about what we're doing, and need to do, that will lead to the results we so dearly desire. This book is about the best practices that have transformed schools across America and how they don't work without a culture of candid and compassionate feedback. Our call to action, as we close, is for leaders to step outside the circle of nice, stop cancelling candor by skirting The What, giving The Out, and posting The Blame, and start living a new leadership life. The next time you're writing feedback to your teachers, call it like it is and clarify the expectations. The next time you're collaborating with your team on a shared decision, be direct with the problem you're trying to solve and hold the people accountable to new and different practices. The next time you're working to grow your teacher leaders, be explicit about the changes they need to make to lead better and follow up to ensure their behaviors are different. Be a leader who pulls no punches but does so with extreme care and respect. Be candid. Be compassionate. Be better. Thank you for reading our book, and we hope you learned something from it.

References

Ackerman, R., Donaldson, G., & Van Der Bogert, R. (1996). *Making sense as a school leader: Persisting questions, creative opportunities*. San Francisco: Jossey-Bass.

Ashkenas, R. (2010). Is your culture too nice? *Harvard Business Review, 8*.

Bambrick-Santoyo, P. (2012). *Leverage leadership: A practical guide to building exceptional schools*. San Francisco: Jossey-Bass.

Berliner, D. & Glass, G. (2014). *50 myths and lies that threaten America's public schools*. New York: Teachers College Press

Blanchard, K., Randolph, A., & Grazier, P. (2007). *Go team! Take your team to the next level*. San Francisco: Berrett-Koehler Publishers, Inc.

Brown, T. (2009). *Change by design: How design thinking transforms organizations and inspires innovation*. New York: HarperCollins Publishers.

Carrol, A. (2014). *The feedback imperative: How to give everyday feedback to speed up your team's success*. Austin, TX: River Grove Books.

Casas, J. (2017). *Culturize: Every student. Every teacher. Every day. Whatever it takes*. San Diego: Dave Burgess Consulting, Inc.

Catmull, E. (2014). *Creativity, Inc.: Overcoming the unforeseen forces that stand in the way of true inspiration*. New York: Random House.

City, E.A., Elmore, R.F., Fiarman, S.E., Teitel, L., & Lachman, A. (2009). *Instructional rounds in education: A network approach to improving teaching and learning*. Boston, MA: Harvard Education Press.

Collins, J. (2001). *Good to great: Why some companies make the leap ... and others don't*. London: Random House.

Covey, S.R. (1989). *The 7 habits of highly effective people: Powerful lessons in personal change*. New York: Simon & Schuster.

Covey, S.R. (2006). *The speed of trust: The one thing that changes everything*. New York: Free Press.

Dalio, R. (2017). *Principles: Life and work*. New York: Simon & Schuster.

Douglas, S. & Sheila, H. (2014). *Thanks for the feedback: The science and art of receiving feedback well.* New York: Penguin Books.

Downey, C.J., Steffy, B.E., English, F.W., Frase, L.E., & Poston, W.K. (2004). *The three-minute classroom walk-through: Changing school supervisory practice one teacher at a time.* Thousand Oaks, CA: Corwin Press.

DuFour, R. & Marzano, R. (2011). *Leaders of learning: How district, school, and classroom leaders improve student achievement.* Bloomington, IN: Solution Tree.

DuFour, R., DuFour, R., Eaker, R., Many, T., & Mattos, M. (2016). *Learning by doing: A handbook for professional learning communities at work.* Bloomington, IN: Solution Tree.

Finley, T. (2014, December 01). 11 Alternatives to "Round Robin" (and "Popcorn") Reading. Retrieved January 25, 2016, from http://www.edutopia.org/blog/alternatives-to-round-robin-reading-todd-finley

Fowler-Fin T. (2013). *Leading instructional rounds in education: A facilitator's guide.* Cambridge, MA: Harvard Education Press.

Fullan, M. (2014). *The principal: Three keys to maximizing impact.* San Francisco: Jossey-Bass.

Gallery Walk. (n.d.). Retrieved from http://www.theteachertoolkit.com/index.php/tool/gallery-walk

Gardner, H. (1991). *The unschooled mind: How children think and how schools should teach.* New York: Basic Books, Inc.

Goodman, N. (n.d.). *Jack Welch on how to manage employees.* Retrieved from https://www.entrepreneur.com/article/224604

Hattie, J. (2009). *Visible learning: A synthesis of over 800 meta-analyses relating to achievement.* New York: Routledge.

Herold, C. (2018). *Vivid vision: A remarkable tool for aligning your business around a shared vision for the future.* Lioncrest Publishing.

Hurley, J.S. (2017). *The one habit: The ultimate guide to increasing engagement and building highly-effective teams.* Scottsdale, AZ: Xmetryx Press.

Kachur, D.S., Stout, J.A., & Edwards, C.L. (2013). *Engaging teachers in classroom walkthroughs.* Alexandria, VA: ASCD.

Kahneman, D. (2011). *Thinking fast and slow.* New York: Farrar, Straus, and Giroux.

Kotter, J. (2014). *Accelerate: Building strategic agility for a faster-moving world.* Boston, MA: Harvard Business School Publishing.

Lanik, M. (2018). *The leader habit: Master the skills you need to lead in just minutes a day.* New York: American Management Association.

Lebowitz, S. (2016, May 20). After overhauling its performance review system, IBM now uses an app to give and receive real-time feedback. *Business Insider.*

Lencioni, P. (2002). *The five dysfunctions of a team: A leadership fable.* San Francisco: Jossey-Bass.

Lencioni, P. (2016). *The ideal team player: How to recognize and cultivate the three essential virtues.* San Francisco: Jossey-Bass.

Levin, L. & Schrum, L. (2017). *Every teacher a leader: Developing the needed dispositions, knowledge, and skills for teacher leadership.* Thousand Oaks, CA: Corwin.

Lockwood, T. & Papke, E. (2018). *Innovation by design. How an organization can leverage design thinking to produce change, drive new ideas, and deliver meaningful solutions.* New York: The Career Press, Inc.

MacDonald, E. (2011). When nice won't suffice: Honest discourse is key to shifting school culture. *Teacher Leadership, 6,* 45–51.

Marzano, R.J. (2003). *What works in schools: Translating research into action.* Alexandria, VA: ASCD.

Marzano, R.J., Pickering, D.J., & Pollock, J.E. (2001). *Classroom instruction that works: Research-based strategies for increasing student achievement.* Alexandria, VA: ASCD.

Maxwell, J.C. (1993). *Developing the leader within you.* Nashville, TN: Thomas Nelson.

Maxwell, J.C. (1998). *The 21 irrefutable laws of leadership: Follow them and people will follow you.* Nashville, TN: Thomas Nelson.

Maxwell, J.C. (2013). *The 17 indisputable laws of teamwork: Embrace them and empower your team.* Nashville, TN: Thomas Nelson.

Morgan, A., Lynch, C., & Lynch, S. (2017). *Spark: How to lead yourself and others to great success.* New York: Houghton Mifflin Harcourt.

Moss, C.M. & Brookhart, S.M. (2015). *Formative classroom walkthroughs: How principals and teachers collaborate to raise student achievement.* Alexandria, VA: ASCD.

Murphy, J.J. (2016). *Pulling together: 10 rules for high-performance teamwork.* Naperville, IL: Simple Truths.

Nawaz, S. (2018). How to create executive team norms—and make them stick. *Harvard Business Review,* January 2018. https://hbr.org/2018/01/how-to-create-executive-team-norms-and-make-them-stick

O'Toole, J. & Bennis, W. (2009). A culture of candor. *Harvard Business Review, 6.*

Patterson, K., Grenny, J., McMillan, R., & Switzler, A. (2012). *Crucial conversations: Tools for talking when stakes are high.* New York: McGraw-Hill.

Peters, T.J., & Waterman, R.H. (1982). *In search of excellence: Lessons from America's best run companies.* New York: Warner Books, Inc.

Ravitch, D. (2014). *Reign of error: The hoax of the privatization movement and the danger to America's public schools.* New York: Vintage Books.

Reeves, D. (2009). *Leading change in your school: How to conquer myths, build commitment, and get results.* Alexandria, VA: ASCD.

Reeves, D. (2016). *From leading to succeeding: The seven elements of effective leadership in education*. Bloomington, IN: Solution Tree.

Roberts, J.E. (2012). *Instructional rounds in action*. Cambridge, MA: Harvard Education Press.

Rock, D. & Grant, H. (2016). Why diverse teams are smarter. *Harvard Business Review*, November 2016. https://hbr.org/2016/11/why-diverse-teams-are-smarter

Scott, K. (2017). *Radical candor: Be a kick-ass both without losing your humanity*. New York: St. Martin's Press.

Sharpe, W. (2009, July 28). Reading Aloud—Is It Worth It? Retrieved January 14, 2016, from http://www.educationworld.com/a_curr/curr213.shtml

Sinek, S. (2011). *Start with why: How great leaders inspire everyone to take action*. New York: Penguin Group.

Skretta, J.A. (2008). *Walkthroughs: A descriptive study of Nebraska high school principal's use of the walkthrough teacher observation process* (Doctoral dissertation). Retrieved from ProQuest.

Smith, S., Chavez, A., & Seaman, G. (2016). *Cognitive growth targets questioning flipbook*. Denver, CO: Magnusson-Skor Publishing LLC.

Spillane, J.P. (2006). *Distributed Leadership*. San Francisco: Jossey-Bass.

Stroh, D.P. (2015). *Systems thinking for social change: A practical guide to solving complex problems, avoiding unintended consequences, and achieving lasting results*. White River Junction, VT: Chelsea Green Publishing.

Sunstein, C.R. & Hastie, R. (2014). *Wiser: Getting beyond groupthink to make groups smarter*. Boston, MA: Harvard Business Review Press.

Teitel, L. (2013). *School-based instructional rounds: Improving teaching and learning across classrooms*. Cambridge, MA: Harvard Education Press.

Tomal, D., Schilling, C., & Wilhite, R. (2014). *The teacher leader: Core competencies and strategies for effective leadership*. London: Rowman & Littlefield.

Whitaker, T. (2013). *What great principals do differently: Eighteen things that matter most*. New York: Routledge.

Whitaker, T. & Gruenert, S. (2015). *School culture rewired: How to define, assess, and transform it*. Alexandria, VA: ASCD.